Dodie Bellamy
is on our mind.

CCA WATTIS INSTITUTE

for CONTEMPORARY ARTS

CONTENTS

Introduction

by ANTHONY HUBERMAN

According to Dodie Bellamy, you can never trust a person with a neat bedroom. The bedroom is a place fraught with conflicting emotions. It's where we go to feel safe and protected, to put our guard down, rest, and build ourselves back up. It's our innermost sanctuary, our last line of defense: when everything feels like it's falling apart, we can always just stay in bed. At the same time, the bedroom is where we go to expose ourselves to others, to test and experiment with what our bodies want and need from and can do to other bodies—which can be soft and sensual but can also get loud, sweaty, and even a bit rough. For those (and many other) reasons, the bedroom needs a door that closes, so that it can be kept separate from the rest of the house. It's where private gets even more private, or, as my aunt Judy likes to say, it's the *indoors indoors.* And even though it's our most familiar place (considering we're there for hours every single day), it's also our most sacred and cherished possession, shared with others only at great personal risk.

Sure, some keep their bedrooms as neat as possible, with clothes put away, bed made, and blankets folded, hoping it can remain calm and orderly. But there is nothing *neat* about our emotional lives—and it's those lives, in all of their uncontrollable furies, that we experience most intensely in the bedroom.

In her writing, Bellamy is constantly contending with the messiness of her emotions. Her aim is never to contain or clean them up but to keep them difficult, uncomfortable, unshapeable. Her own *Barf Manifesto* (2008) makes it crystal clear: she wants an art of excess, one that says too much, where "meaning is so surplus it decimates form," and/or the other way around: where "form is so vicious it beats the fucking pony of content to bits." The Barf describes her literary form: "feminist, unruly, cheerfully monstrous . . . an upheaval, born of our hangover from imbibing too much Western Civ." It makes a mess of meaning.

To barf (or vomit, puke, heave, hurl, throw up, you name it) points to a fragility: it comes from the body, is *of* the body but is too much for it, is rejected by the body, and therefore erupts from it, whether we like it or not. It represents a threat—most people don't want to see it, or at least not out in the open. Barf is far too horrifying and abject for that. At the same time, it shares a lot in common with *the passionate*, as opposed to *the intellectual*: it doesn't come loaded with self-consciousness or moral superiority but only with force and materiality. It doesn't have good or bad intentions, nor does it have right or wrong opinions. It simply *happens*, inevitably, like shit. Or like laughter.

The metaphor of a literary Barf works so well for Bellamy because what she's after, in her own words, is to *enact the feral*. She wants to rip narrative out of its domesticated form and *rewild* it, no matter how menacing that might be. In that sense, the Barf is a sign of strength, not weakness: it indicates a willingness to remain raw, vulnerable, exposed, and subject to the judgment of others. And so Bellamy proceeds to love too much and to say too much. This is her feminism, her political stance: to empower the wild and the *too much*. In her mind, a good essay should always embarrass its author a bit.

As a result, when Bellamy is faced with a problem, she exaggerates the problem. When she feels vulnerable, she exposes herself. When she gets humiliated, she tells everyone. When she is faced with her own body's limitations, she "ram[s] it down my readers' throats." In *Academonia* (2006), she confesses that "there are things that are wrong with me. I'm a woman. I write about sex. I'm too old. I'm too weird. I'm white. I'm a white woman who's too old to write about sex." As Kaye Mitchell argues in her piece included in this publication, shame is not something Bellamy tries to overcome but something she works to immerse herself in. She pushes humiliation as far as it will stretch until it flips over and becomes arousal. She calls it "an erotics of disclosure."

It's important to clarify that Bellamy doesn't see her work as transgressive or radical. She's not trying to convince anyone, least of all with anything resembling rational arguments, sincerity, morality, coherence, or "truth," whatever that means. She sees so-called "sophistication" as something that can only get in the way. She's more interested in subverting what's considered "important" subject matter. Her writing, at least in part, comes from the unconscious or the impulsive, which are often too vulgar and too barfy to form a single acceptable message. Instead, she's interested in how the sexual consumes and devours rationality, making it impossible—how the physicality of sex will always elude language. Therefore, inspired by her friend Kathy Acker, she doesn't write poems or novels *about* sex but imagines ways the writing itself could contain a sexual force. For both Acker and Bellamy, stealing or appropriating language from others is a libidinal process that satisfies an urge to take, suck, and consume other people. In each sentence, words grab and clutch on to other words, fearlessly but also desperately, no matter how traumatic some might be. In Bellamy's work, language feels hungry, potentially insatiable, as if it were trying to sink its teeth into our necks, like the vampire-protagonist of her first novel, *The Letters of Mina Harker* (1998). Her body is always entangled with ours.

Dodie Bellamy's writing is dangerous in the way addictions are dangerous: readers will find it impossible to keep themselves at a safe distance from her words.

As you'll discover in the essays in this book, Bellamy's work and life fall outside of most norms. She grew up in the Midwest, in the 1950s and '60s, the first member of her family ever to go to college—and her complex relationships to notions of class, and to migrating from one class to another, remain central to her artistic voice and sensibility. Her sexual life began early, at age eleven, in a relationship with another woman that would last fifteen years. Feeling lost and alienated, she found herself joining a cult, an experience she would subsequently write about in her book *TV Sutras* (2014). *Dada, Surrealism and their Heritage*, a 1968 exhibition at the Art Institute of Chicago, made an early and lasting impression. At twenty-seven, in 1978, she moved to San Francisco, where Kathleen Fraser, at San Francisco State University, recommended she join Bob Glück's writing workshop at Small Press Traffic, which would soon become the birthplace of New Narrative. Along with a small group of other (mostly gay) poets such as Steve Abbott, Bruce Boone, Gail Scott, Gabrielle Daniels, and Camille Roy, Bellamy gave shape to a queer avant-garde that contested the Language Poets and their proclamations about the end of language, the end of content, the death of the author. New Narrative, more than anything, was an assertion that narrative was not dead and that many stories remained untold—mostly those from perspectives outside the racial or sexual mainstream. Breaking everyone's rules—both those of the "academy" and those of the 1980s literary avant-garde—the New Narrative poets wrote about sex and gossip, spilling it all out. As a result, they strengthened their sense of community, especially in the face of the AIDS epidemic, forming close interpersonal bonds via shared language and shared narratives. New Narrative marked a rebirth of the author.

Among the New Narrative writers was Kevin Killian, a gay poet and playwright from Long Island. He and Bellamy would ultimately marry and become life partners—up until just a few months ago, when Killian tragically fell victim to cancer. Bellamy's text for this book was, in fact, a coping mechanism that the two invented shortly after Killian's diagnosis: a strategy to project a future, to imagine being alive for a full year. Each week, for twelve months, they would take turns choosing a topic and write one thousand words. By the seventh week, they found themselves writing in Killian's hospital room. Bellamy finished the text alone.

Before reaching such a touching and tragic climax, this book begins with a long essay by Megan Milks. Given the prompt to write a *New Yorker*-like profile of Bellamy, Milks spent an extended amount of time researching, reading, interviewing, and getting to know their subject in-depth. They visited Bellamy's papers at Yale University's Beinecke Rare Book and Manuscript Library and chose the images that appear throughout this volume. Andrew Durbin's essay began as a lecture he gave at the CCA Wattis Institute in September 2018, and adds his own personal take on Bellamy's work, complete with the right amount of embarrassing anecdotes. Kaye Mitchell's text first appeared in a 2018 book of essays related to shame and modern writing, and contributes a more detached and analytic perspective on Bellamy's work.

Most of all, this book is the result of tireless work and incredible commitment on the part of Jeanne Gerrity, deputy director and head of publications at the Wattis. And Wayne Smith, a close and old friend of Bellamy's, proved to be the perfect graphic designer for the project.

From September 2018 to August 2019, Bellamy's work and ideas were the subject of, and departure point for, the fifth yearlong research season at the Wattis, where a single artist becomes the focus of an extended period of attention and forms the basis of a collective conversation that expands outwards to encompass broader themes and questions in the fields of art, literature, film, politics, and philosophy, among others. We began as a small reading group: Nicole Archer, Michele Carlson, Tonya Foster, Jeanne Gerrity, Lisa Heinis, Glen Helfand, Trista Mallory, Anne McGuire, K.r.m. Mooney, and Marcela Pardo Ariza, each of whom brought new ideas and thoughtful insights to our monthly discussions. We then expanded to a monthly series of public events at the Wattis, with artists such as Frances Stark and Mike Kuchar, a night of stand-up comedians hosted by writers Tara Jepsen and Michelle Tea, and theorists such as Jack Halberstam, among many others. Finally, this book extends our reach further still to all those who find it, thanks to the help of our co-publishers Semiotext(e).

To all of those mentioned, and to many others who aren't mentioned by name, I owe my deepest gratitude. And most of all, to Dodie: thank you—this is for you.

Dodie Bellamy's Crude Genius

by MEGAN MILKS

D odie Bellamy is wearing a dark shirt that says "Witch Camp" in a blue bubble when I meet her for community acupuncture. On one pocket of her matte-black backpack, a gold pin urges "Change Everything." We don't hug.

That's for the best: I'm sick. I flew into San Francisco with a bad head cold, and the descent left a swell of pressure in my right ear. I'm also nervous, daunted by the task ahead. How does one profile someone who has so thoroughly examined herself? Over nine books, several chapbooks, and many, many essays, Bellamy has mined her life to brilliant effect, her writing swiveling inward and out to address sex, desire, gender, class, digital life, language, the politics of aesthetics—and illness. *Cough.* Having read nearly all of it, I could sketch a rough portrait right now. The Dodie I know is an outlaw, a rule breaker, a provocateur: among other transgressions, she has "cunted" the *Norton Anthology of Poetry* (see *Cunt Norton*, where she combines Chaucer, Spencer, and so on with porno-erotic texts). Her audacity is curtailed, or more often driven, by an undercurrent of abject embarrassment ("my crap's all wrong," she laments in *Barf Manifesto*'s infamous toilet scene, "too much for Eileen's plumbing").[1] The Dodie I know is frankly intimate, cannily crude, and very, very funny. If she can be difficult, moody, at times socially challenged ("One therapist told me I had 'reverse charisma,'" she remarks in "The Feminist Writers' Guild"),[2] she uses writing to sit in these moments and spread out. She's a gossip, a brilliant commentator on art and life. The Dodie I know knows herself extremely well and has been profiling that self ruthlessly for much of her life.

The on-the-page Dodie is more concentrated, of course, wound up in, inseparable from the time and space of writing, a loose constraint Bellamy manipulates with numerous strategies to varying effects. From the giddy excesses of her first novel, *The Letters of Mina Harker* (1998), to the conceptual pornography of *Cunt-Ups* (2001) and *Cunt Norton* (2013), from the procedural New Age kitsch of *The TV Sutras* (2014), to the virtuosic range of her most recent essay collection, *When the Sick Rule the World* (2015), Bellamy is an endlessly inventive writer. Her formal experiments balance intellectual rigor with a queer feminist commitment to mess and play. Though hardly a genre loyalist, she's best known for her work with the essay, which she seems to reinvent again and again. Knitting together art, ideas, and reportage in startling combinations, her prose achieves a dense and dizzying velocity. "It's graceful and beautiful," says peer and publisher Chris Kraus. "As I see it, Dodie Bellamy is one of the most important living American writers."

She's also one of the most underrecognized. In fact, to say that she is as underrecognized as she is influential would be uncontroversial, I think. That she was selected as the subject of the 2018–2019 research season at the CCA Wattis Institute for Contemporary Arts is the kind of overdue appreciation that has largely eluded her. Her enormous contributions to experimental prose—even at this moment, when "creative nonfiction" has exploded as a field—have not translated to major awards, grants, or even a solid teaching gig.

At Circle Community Acupuncture, the Barcaloungers form a big ring, all but two occupied by reclining guests swathed in a hodgepodge of blankets and bedsheets—rocket ships on florals on solids. Melissa the acupuncturist gets me situated, then leaves to tend to Bellamy, who has settled into a chair on the other side of the room. For a long while, I resist reclining, wheeling my scrutiny around like the journalist I'm supposed to be. Then I realize I'm infringing on the space: not journalist but voyeur. I find the lever to release the footrest.

Melissa returns and whispers questions about my state and needs. "My right ear is clogged from the flight," I tell her. "I'm getting over a cold." That's optimistic. She places a needle in the soft dent behind the lobe as someone begins snoring blissfully. "That's Dodie," Melissa says affectionately. "She usually goes about forty minutes."

"How do you feel?" Bellamy asks after our session. "Good," I say, harnessing the power of positive thinking. "Relaxed. A little off-kilter." The clog has traveled from my right ear to my left. We're on our way to Basil Canteen, a nearby Thai restaurant where, over blistered green beans, we lean in close and trade notes on shared acquaintances. We chat amiably about last year's New Narrative conference, then turn to some recent kerfuffles within the Bay Area poetry community. She's more guarded than I expected, though I sense a strong impulse to share. "This is off the record," she says before launching in. I nod, understanding the boundary though somewhat disappointed by it. New Narrative, the school of writing with which Bellamy is closely associated, was so much about installing this kind of gossip into the literary record—as is so much of her work. (Eileen Myles on *The Letters of Mina Harker*: "Dodie Bellamy writes brilliant gossip and if there's anything better than literature this is it."[3]) But rumors circulate differently in the age of social media. My friend Grace recently gave me a soap labeled "GOSSIP STOPPER." I'll soak it up, but the gossip stops here. (*Psst*: Bellamy's recent essay in *Eleven Eleven* gets into some of it.)

Bellamy has always had an impulse to tell, tell; as a child, she was reproached for it. "Don't feel you have to tell me everything," she recalls her mother saying. She spent her childhood reading books and sort of "wallowing around," she explains to me, in stark contrast to her mother, who endorsed a working-class toughness and had little patience for demonstrative behavior. "I loved her deeply. But we didn't like each other at all. I was everything she disapproved of," Bellamy says, laughing. "I was totally emotional." She would eventually learn to exploit this effusiveness in her work to powerful effect. "I favor a direct assault of over-the-top emotion," she wrote in 2004, "hysteria even."[4] And gossip, though seen as a "low art," she concluded, is "a labor of disenfranchised subjectivity."[5]

Throughout her career, Bellamy has railed against social and aesthetic classism: eschewing the bourgeois and genteel in favor of the vulgar and the grotesque. This critical stance has been shaped indelibly by her working-class upbringing in Hammond, Indiana, a suburb of Chicago. Her mother, Winifred "Winnie" Bellamy, worked in the school cafeteria; her father, Byron "Barney" Bellamy, was a carpenter from a long line of union carpenters. Her only sibling, a younger brother named Joey, left high school after falling in with peers involved in petty crime, eventually taking a job in the local steel mill. (Their first real talk as adults, Bellamy has written, took place at their father's funeral. Their parents

"'did some job of raising kids,' Joey joked. 'I'm a convicted felon, and you're weird.'"[6]) While her mother was "totally happy to be working class," she says, her father had some shame around it. "He was really smart," she tells me, "which I don't think was in his favor. He always felt kind of ashamed of his position in life." Though he valued education and encouraged Bellamy's studies, he himself quit school after seventh grade and read only one book in his life, *The Jungle Book*, by Rudyard Kipling.

Bellamy describes her relationship with him as "horrible." He was verbally abusive and "totally sexually inappropriate," she says. "He was always telling me how disgusting I was. Sometimes he would call me 'it.' He was really mean. And unfortunately, he was also very handsome." To him she traces her "deep streak of masochism" as well as her relationship to crudeness and obscenity.

"I think both the elegance and shockingness of Dodie's work seem to be about her class relation," said Myles, who shares with Bellamy a working-class background, albeit regionally different. "Part of the thing of feeling like you don't belong in a room is that you're kind of like, 'Oh, yeah, you think I don't belong here, well, I'll *show* you I don't belong here.'" In Bellamy, Myles said, this manifests as a "boundary-busting sharing of bodily or personal content."

Bruce Boone, an early mentor of Bellamy's, described readings where "Dodie will just do a deliberate crudity, and it will be very refreshing. It's a nice puncture of a balloon."

At the same time, Myles said, "She's a beautiful writer, and she knows it. I think it's hard-won and comes from intense reading and studying literature. She's a very unofficial scholar."

Her class status has been fraught for Bellamy. In her adolescence, she wanted desperately to be middle class. She was the first in her family to attend college, which created more friction between her and her mother. "She thought that I thought that I was better than her," she tells me. "And when I was younger, that was true." This changed when Bellamy got a job working in the library at Indiana University Bloomington. "I started hating middle-class people. I could see how disgusting they were. It made me start appreciating the values of my parents. They're very honest people. You could trust them. You knew where you stood." Though she has since, through education and career, attained middle-class status—Semiotext(e) publisher-Hedi El Kholti calls her a "class transfuge"—she retains a strong working-class identity.

At the age of eleven, Bellamy became romantically involved with a neighbor, Janis. She was "this predatory girl who was coming on to all the girls at all the pajama parties," she tells me. They became girlfriends in an open-secret kind of way (though they were kicked out of Girl Scouts, she says, for being lesbians) and stayed together until Bellamy was twenty-six. "We had the same relationship dynamic we had when we were eleven," she says. "It was a really fucked-up, unhealthy relationship." To some extent, it was as though her thwarted desires to be close with her mother were transferred to Janis, who eagerly fulfilled them. "People do not hug me," Bellamy says wryly. "But I can fuse like you would not believe."

Bellamy has searched for community and new forms of belonging throughout her adult life. In 1969 Bellamy enrolled in IU with Janis, and they moved to Bloomington together. While working toward her degree in Comparative Literature, Bellamy and Janis joined Eckankar, a spiritual group—she calls it a cult—their senior year. Eckankar emerged out of the alternative religious movement of the 1960s and was among the most successful groups, attracting tens of thousands of members. "I was dysfunctionally shy, a borderline agoraphobic, afraid to talk to salesladies in department stores," Bellamy wrote in a 1995 exposé on the group. "As Eckankar filled my life, I felt like I was entering Shangri-la; a new glistening world of love, of possibility opened before me."[7]

She committed to Eckankar for a decade, enjoying the acceptance, the community, and the sex. "For ten years this was my life," she writes in "Cultured," the long essay that closes *The TV Sutras*, "for ten years I was gone."[8] She finally left in the early 1980s, after evidence of founder Paul Twitchell's plagiarisms of other religious texts came to light. By that time, she had found new community upon moving to San Francisco. (Eckankar is still active—Janis, Bellamy's ex, is now a higher initiate.)

Prior to that consequential move, Bellamy was stuck in a kind of holding pattern with Janis. When Janis stayed on at IU for graduate school, Bellamy did the same, eventually completing two master's degrees in Education. "We were constantly breaking up," Bellamy tells me. "I was constantly trying to get out of the relationship." When they finally split for good after finishing graduate school and moving to Chicago, Bellamy realized she had skipped whole layers of emotional development. "I had never individuated in certain ways." Janis, aggressively a caretaker, had managed Bellamy's emotions for fifteen years. "If I was upset, I had no inner resources on how to take care of myself. I couldn't do self-soothing. So I ended up having panic attacks."

Bellamy moved to San Francisco not long after their breakup, following some of her gay friends from college. It was the fall of

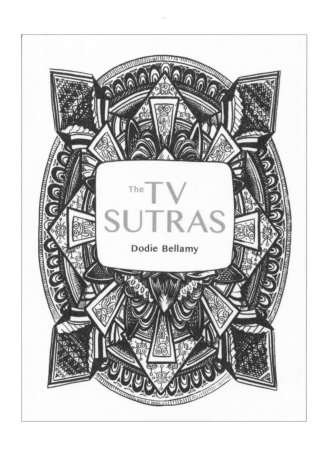

The TV SUTRAS

Dodie Bellamy

1978, a month before the murder of Harvey Milk. She was twenty-seven, still involved in Eckankar, and struggling with boundaries and emotional regulation.

"During that time," she says, "several people told me that I was the most insecure person they'd ever met." This was before she started seriously writing. "I always wanted to write," Bellamy tells me. "I was very shy about it. It wasn't until I moved out here, and I was living alone, and I was terrified—and had what seemed like endless amounts of time on my hands—then all I did was write."

She also searched for literary community, attending readings "indiscriminately." She became involved in the Bay Area chapter of the Feminist Writers' Guild, an experience she's written about a few times: first with scornful distance and later with grateful admiration. In 1979 Bellamy formed a publishing collective with other guild members and put out an anthology titled *Danaid*. In her more recent essay on the group, included in *When the Sick Rule the World*, she recalls the debates they had over how to assess women's writing, appreciating the overtness with which they were critiquing classism and aesthetic hierarchies. Though Bellamy eventually found herself magnetized to the hipper, more intellectual community of feminist and queer writers in San Francisco, the kinship she found in the guild was formative. "Never again would I receive such uncomplicated acceptance from a community," she writes. "Never again would my vacant stares, weirdness, social dysfunction be held with such tenderness; never again would I experience an arts community whose mandate was inclusivity."[9]

At the suggestion of a friend in the guild, Bellamy began auditing graduate classes at San Francisco State University with experimental feminist poet Kathleen Fraser, who became an invaluable mentor.

Combined with her time in the guild and her own self-education in feminist literature, the courses gave Bellamy firm anchorage in the critical feminism that has shaped her body of work—a framework foregrounding the female body and its politics.

Meanwhile, Bellamy got together with her first husband, Sergio Santiago, who was also part of Eckankar. They had met through a mutual friend in San Francisco, but it wasn't until they ran into each other at a New Year's Eve party in Chicago that they talked at length. They spent an exhilarating month together over the winter holidays. After a brief return to San Francisco, Bellamy moved to Chicago to be with Santiago. They married in 1981.

During this time, Bellamy had a bad drug experience that affected her for years. "I was hanging out with Debbie from [my story] 'The Debbies I Have Known,' and we smoked this marijuana that she got from this porn dealer friend of hers. We stayed high for two days, and I had drug flashbacks for five years after that. It was clearly laced." The experience left her poisoned and destabilized. "I was having hallucinations and racing energy up the spine," she explains. "I really didn't know if I was ever going to be normal again. It seemed like it was teetering. Just one little bit more and I would have been psychotic." She learned to rely on breathing exercises and other forms of grounding to cope with the flashbacks; acupuncture also helped.

After nine months in Chicago, Bellamy returned with Santiago to San Francisco, where she reconnected with Fraser, who continued to encourage Bellamy's writing and funneled her into the workshops Robert Glück had been leading at Small Press Traffic. ("The fact that there're any women involved in New Narrative," says Bellamy, "is mostly because of Kathleen Fraser.") Located in Noe Valley, these free weekly workshops had already become the epicenter of a literary movement known as New Narrative: a transgressive, self- and body-obsessed, queer avant-garde that formed in part against the anti-narrative, self-evacuating Language poetry that was dominant in the Bay Area at the time. Combining the confessional with the conceptual, New Narrative experimented with the possibilities of loosely autobiographical storytelling to produce an exploded and unstable "I." At the same time, having grown out of second-wave feminism and the gay rights movement, it was as community focused as it was narcissistic: "a writing prompted not by fiat nor consensus, nor by the totalizing suggestions of the MFA 'program era,' but by community," write Bellamy and Kevin Killian in their introduction to *Writers Who Love Too Much*, an anthology of New Narrative writing. "It would be unafraid of experiment, unafraid of kitsch, unafraid of sex and gossip and political debate."[10] Bellamy had found a home.

"It was a really beautiful moment in my life," she reflects. "I was in this bubble, this community." She developed close relationships with both Glück and Boone; while the former acted as an informal mentor to various members of the workshop, Bellamy gravitated toward the latter. Boone was considered more introverted and esoteric than Glück; he also holds a PhD from University of California, Berkeley. "I studied postmodernism and stuff, and she's a real theory gal. She was a force of nature," he recalled. "She knew what she wanted. She wanted to be a writer. She discovered a group of us who were quote unquote—no, for real—writers (as opposed to commercial or something), and she stormed the house."

For Boone, the "towering trait" that set Bellamy apart was her objective self-scrutiny. He quoted Heraclitus, the fifth-century BCE philosopher, to me over the phone. "One of his sayings was, 'I went in search of myself.' And 'When I follow the soul I never reach its boundaries. Wherever I go, it goes further.' When I read Dodie, I get a sense that examining herself is always scrutinizing the lives, first, of other women, then—everyone. She reads a lot of theory, and there's this philosophical bent in her."

"It's just wonderful," he went on, describing her writing. "The faculties of imagination and intellect combining with the personal and yet utterly ruthless and objective, and at the same time funny, skipping from genre to genre as she goes."

As Bellamy became immersed in the writing community, she and Santiago grew apart. "He was just totally inappropriate for me," she tells me. "He hardly talked. I knew when I got together with him that it was a mistake. He offered nothing. No emotional support. Not that he didn't want to; he just wasn't going to do it. But I think it was really good for me in this sense of learning to take care of myself, to have this container." After four years of marriage, they amicably divorced.

The weekly workshops at Small Press Traffic attracted a vibrant constellation of other local writers, including Camille Roy, Marsha Campbell, Michael Amnasan, Sam D'Allesandro, and a young writer who'd recently arrived from Long Island: Kevin Killian. He and Bellamy married in 1986.

They made an unlikely pair, as Killian was gay, and Bellamy's sexual identity was ambiguously queer. Bellamy recalls not taking him seriously at first: his persona then was "happy-boy clownish, drunken." One night she was having an anxiety attack brought on by a drug flashback, and Killian took her home and held her through it.

After that, she felt she could trust him, and they grew close. "It was just an accident of fate," she tells me. "He was not a good choice, obviously. He was an alcoholic homosexual who couldn't be in a relationship." She laughed. (Killian quit drinking shortly after they married.) "It was kind of based on the fact that we could talk, which I really needed. I could tell him anything."

"She was very talented," Killian said, recalling his own first impressions. "She did a lot of drinking. She was in excess in a lot of ways. Partly that was the time." He had moved to San Francisco in the early 1980s to finish his dissertation in literature and quickly found himself pulled into the energies of the Bay Area. "It was a time when the great pioneers of gay writing, queer writing, were *still alive*. And they were often in San Francisco, so we would get to meet these legends." He rattles off names: Allen Ginsberg, William Burroughs, Judy Grahn, Adrienne Rich. Many of the Berkeley Language poets organized panels at local venues. There were exhilarating conversations around feminism and lesbianism, too, with talks and panels happening constantly. "It was all very heady for a young writer."

This was also the heyday of gay cruising in San Francisco. "You could have sex four or five times a day," he recalled. "Just cruising on the streets, and everyone was saying, yes, why not, because we didn't realize that AIDS was around the corner. Then everything in life and in writing changed."

It was during the early days of AIDS that Killian and Bellamy got together. "We had been very close, and we had thought we should just get married, and then Dodie would get the insurance that she needed. And then this extra thing of having sex was like a lagniappe"—an added plus, and a surprise to Killian, who "was not the type of gay boy to have sex with a lot of women." They entered into an open marriage. After her claustrophobic fifteen years with Janis, Bellamy was eager to explore.

"As soon as we were married, she began having affairs with a number of different men," he said. She fictionalizes these relationships in *The Letters of Mina Harker*, an epistolary work that took nearly a decade to write. The novel's premise is that Bellamy has been possessed by *Dracula*'s victim-turned-vampire Mina Harker. Mina pursues liaisons with a number of men who become the subjects of letters to her friends and include Boone (as Dr. Van Helsing) and D'Allesandro.[11] Mina/Dodie's zigzagging tour through her sexual rampages is underpinned by passages lifted from other writers such as Georges Bataille, David Wojnarowicz, and Sylvia Plath. Charged with multidirectional eros, the voice of Mina is scandalously, uproariously over the top. ("Dear Reader, I could fuck you better if I knew what you look like.")[12] Her lovers are pseudonymized as Quincey, Dion, and Rendezvous, but it's not hard to figure out who they are. As Mina, Bellamy also dramatizes numerous sex scenes with a wry, hapless KK (the fictionalized Killian).

"I'm at the end of *The Letters of Mina Harker*," Killian said, "crouching above her on my hands and knees, and I say, 'This is what you always wanted, isn't it, a house that talks.'" He smiled. "It all worked out pretty well."

Effusively citational, frankly sexual, and slyly confessional, *The Letters of Mina Harker* exemplifies how Bellamy oriented New Narrative's trademark commingling of the personal with the theoretical around female subjectivity and desire. "There was all this work that came out of that scene that was really very sexual, but no women were writing that work," said writer Diana Cage, who was Bellamy's assistant when she directed Small Press Traffic in the mid-1990s. "And then Dodie was. And it was so great. It wasn't just sexual; it was embodied. She was solving this problem of how you describe female sexual aggression—what does it mean to be a desiring female body."

Myles was heavily influenced by Bellamy's early work, including early excerpts from *Mina*. "Her use of pastiche seemed ahead of the pack in a certain way, and I saw that instantly in the '80s. She was doing something different, something special. Even something simple like how she maneuvered italics in a text—stuff like that's huge." Myles calls Bellamy a master of pastiche—"of wrangling and herding ideas and movements in a text."

"I want that sense of an alien voice," Bellamy wrote of her appropriations in *Mina*, "all authoritarian with sharp edges to threaten the confessional, colloquial tone of my 'regular' writing. . . . I want that sense of a language that is not mine coming in, a language that I can read but never own, a language that I don't want to own. . . . I rip the language of the academy out of context and force it into my own writing, so it can turn up its nose at my noisy corporeality. My vulgarity surrounds it on all sides, with huge slimy cunt teeth ready to snap elitism in two."[13]

When I ask her about *The Letters of Mina Harker*, Bellamy laments its limbo status with the University of Wisconsin Press, which won't revert the rights to her but have never done anything to promote it. "I feel like people forgot that book. And if people knew about it, it would have a new audience. Don't you think?"

I agree and share that I recently ran into poet Kay Gabriel at my community health center with a copy of *Mina* in her hand. (I later asked Gabriel about her relationship to the book. "A couple years ago," she wrote in an email, "I started writing a manuscript of letters and found *Mina Harker* delivering the genre's secrets to my apartment, no signature required. Like: despite the addressee, the letter's a ruse for writing in the first-person singular, the more selfish the better. . . . The excesses of genre—pornography, body horror—turn into a kind of realism, locked in a staring contest with a history drenched in shit.")

Our conversation about *Mina* leads to a conversation about writing sex. "*Mina* was really hard to get published," Bellamy tells me. "It was rejected by a lot of people." Someone at New Directions who had championed the book confided in a memo that the explicit content posed a problem for the editors. ("It will be a cold day in Hell," the note quotes one editor as saying, "before this much sex makes it into a ND book.") "The best things about my writing have often been seen as a problem," she says with nonchalance. "I got so much shit for writing about sex. And not taken seriously. That people can do this now—like all the experimental poets who are putting blowjobs into their poems—they should understand that that wasn't always the case."

Cage offered similar observations. "Even the way that people talk about female desire now," she said, or the way it's shown on TV: "There are actually desiring female characters all the time, and it's really ethical and sexy. We take it for granted now. In the '90s we didn't take it for granted. Dodie is the first place where I actually understood that it was a thing that needed to be described. She was thinking about things that the rest of us were having trouble articulating."

For Myles, too, Bellamy is a vanguard, "always, always leading the way" when it comes to writing sex. "She's the female practitioner of sex writing whose work I've maybe read the most of and think is probably the most awesome. I mean Kathy [Acker] wrote about sex. Lots of people do. There's just something—the affrontery, the luridness, the pleasure, the kind of necessity. It seems like survival in Dodie's work. And sex *is* survival—for cultures, and not about reproduction, but about presence and being here and radical lives."

Chris Kraus highlighted the "avariciousness" of Bellamy's writing about sexuality. "It's not strategic. It wants everything. It's consuming. By giving her particular form of desire visibility, she gives permission to the whole world to be truthful in their own particularities and—" she searches for the right word. "Unredeemable. Everyone is unredeemable if you get down to it, and Dodie is so unapologetic about being unredeemable that in the end it gets redeemed."

After *Mina*, Bellamy published *Cunt-Ups* (2001), a work of conceptual poetry composed of primarily pornographic texts, her "cunt-up" method riffing on Burroughs and Gysin's cut-up technique. The result is a delirious genderfuckery as bodies swap genitals and *you* becomes *I*. It's a tremendously porous, exhilarating text that seems to actually pant: "The parts that feel best to me are my male difference and my vagina. . . . Then I grew and became an old cock, tip arched orange."[14] The sex in Bellamy's prose is never strictly hot, nor is it aimed at empowerment. It's ambivalent, braced, confusing, funny, unsettling, weird, and thoroughly, gleefully queer. And, especially in *Cunt-Ups*, you cannot forget it is made out of language.

Cage remembers Bellamy's work from this period upsetting other students in her classes at SFSU. "We would read her work, and anytime you would have anybody who wasn't queer or whatever, they would feel so *upset* about it. They would be *angry*."

In 2013 Bellamy published *Cunt Norton*, which applies the cunt-up tactic to the 1975 edition of the *Norton Anthology of Poetry*. ("Gender is nothing compared to this book," Ariana Reines writes in her foreword. "This could be the most joyful book on Earth.")[15]

Cunt-Ups, which is getting a seventeenth-anniversary reissue in fall 2019, was written when Bellamy was in her forties. Throughout her career she has challenged the compulsory desexualization of the middle-aged (and up) woman. She still is. For her talk at the Wattis Institute at the opening event for the 2018–2019 research season dedicated to her, she read from *The Fourth Form*, an old, abandoned novel that she's recently returned to, about an online romance that leads to fleshy encounters. The book revels in language as desire and fantasy as sex. Here's a taste: "The bed was our movie screen *flesh dissolves, action dissolves* the X-rays from my tremendous ego shrink his cock to the size of a microbe and Ed's cock goes on a *Fantastic Voyage*. As I climax in tidal wave convulsions, sticky fluids suck Ed's miniature cock through the cervix's puffy hole and into my bloodstream. Iridescent blue and red blobs exchange gasses. This is the miracle of life."[16] Afterward she told me she felt vulnerable reading it aloud, aware of its "impropriety" coming from a woman in her sixties. I was surprised by this confession; she's been resisting such proprieties for years. But being critical of sexist and ageist attitudes doesn't mean being immune to their effects.

In her 2004 essay "Low Culture," Bellamy wrote, "In a gay culture, where there is a vocabulary for talking about sex, my work doesn't

feel all that transgressive. But then place the same work within
a straight world, with all those things one doesn't talk about 'in
mixed company,' and I become a pervert."[17] In Cage's view, this
kind of context-dependent reception is one reason among many
that Bellamy has been underrecognized: "She was before her time.
She's a woman. She's not straight in the sense that we all think of as
straight. If you were a lesbian, you could at least be sexualized and
objectified in this way, so she didn't have that because she wasn't
that. There was no sexual scene for her to fit into. She straddled all
these different scenes and worlds, and none of it worked in her favor.
She totally got overlooked and is underappreciated."

In the bio on her website, Bellamy declares herself "not a prizes
and awards type writer" before listing an SF Goldie Award in
Literature and a Firecracker Award for *Cunt-Ups*: modest recognition
for someone who has been publishing significant, game-changing
work for so long.[18] But the literary awards system tends to reify genre
boundaries and favor quiet, lyrical prose, a mode antithetical to
Bellamy's. "I stopped applying for grants. I have all this writing
now that doesn't have any sex in it," she says, bemused. "Maybe
I should try again."

I meet Bellamy at the rent-controlled apartment she shares with
Killian, on Minna Street, in San Francisco's South of Market
district. She's lived here since 1991. It's a third-floor walkup, no
buzzer, and I'm apologetic for having made her come all the way
down, only to go all the way up again. There's a new bottlebrush
tree in front of the building, she points out. "Isn't it hideous?" It's
also extremely allergenic, she tells me.

Their apartment is stuffed to the gills. In the living room, there are books upon books, two deep in the broad shelving units that line the longest walls. The short hallway into the kitchen is dwarfed by twin floor-to-ceiling bookcases jammed full. The other main feature is art: stacked, leaning, hanging. Killian gives me a quick run-through. Propped on the molding, a Phoebe Gloeckner portrait of Killian keeps company with a Colter Jacobsen drawing of Bellamy. He shows me work by Joe Brainard, Etel Adnan, Seth Price, Marcus Ewert ("the last person to have sex with Burroughs," he shares, "at the age of seventeen"), Raymond Pettibon, Xylor Jane, Elijah Burgher, and many others. There's a beloved framed photograph of Killian with Dennis Cooper in their shared office and one of Kathy Acker's dresses photographed by Kaucyila Brooke (as described by Bellamy in "Digging Through Kathy Acker's Stuff": "a simple stretchy black dress that [Kaucyila] stuffed so it's awkward and misshapen. . . . I find the photo sweet and a bit pathetic. Perfect.")[19] More art, more books (*The Limits of Autobiography* by Leigh Gilmore, among others) in the tiny half-bathroom off the office. All surfaces in creative use.

"Oh, it's crazy," Matias Viegener, a close friend, says of their apartment. "It's wild. It's pretty chaotic. I don't think they care, to be frank."

I'm amazed that Bellamy can squeeze up to a dozen people in the living room for her renowned summer workshop, but I imagine the intimacy is part of the experience. I'll be meeting some of the participants tonight, at a Wattis reading featuring Bellamy's former students. ("The apartment is like another workshop member," says Michele Carlson, who organized the event.) It's a beloved space. Art from their collection has been displayed at the Manhattan nonprofit White Columns as part of a reading room exhibition; it's also featured in the book *The Bigness of Things: New Narrative and Visual Culture* (2017).

I've been sifting through Bellamy and Killian's combined archives at the Beinecke Library at Yale, delighting in pulling out tacky Valentine's Day and Christmas birthday cards (Bellamy's birthday is on Valentine's Day; Killian's on Christmas Eve), while the other researchers manipulate delicate pages with gloves. Here's Bellamy scowling, in costume to perform in a play by Jack Spicer; here's a large photograph of Killian from behind, standing nude and unassuming in a doorframe ("Kevin's backside," reads the caption scrawled on the back). It is unusual for two living writers to combine their papers in this way, but it makes sense given how intertwined their lives and work are. I find a friendship contract signed by Killian and Bellamy in 1985. "Re: Friendship between DB & KK," it reads. "We will be friends together, no matter who or what or who [sic] comes between us because they can't touch it." Under their signatures are two thumbprints in dried blood.

"They're so fun together," says Cage. "If they have any animosity toward each other, I've never seen it exhibited, ever." They're also an unusual couple: "Part of it is because Kevin is a gay man, and Dodie's sexuality is, who knows, grab bag." They're not a traditional romantic couple, she goes on, then corrects herself—"They are, they definitely are. But there's something extra." I wonder if this "something extra" has to do with how they circulate both individually and as a couple, in their writing and in the community.

From 1992 to 2005, Bellamy and Killian co-published the monthly zine *Mirage #4/PERIOD[ICAL]*. Of *Mirage* Bellamy has said: "We wanted to create a forum for a writing community that was inclusive, not exclusionary"—taking a page from that feminist publishing collective she formed in the late 1970s—"to recontextualize the work of prestigious writers by jamming them up against unknown, beginning, or, frankly, nonwriters . . . to invent a new economy of reading." Charles Bernstein notoriously called *Mirage* the absolute low end of high art, which, Bellamy says on her website, "we take as a compliment." The project was recently revived for twelve issues as part of the Wattis research season.

When Viegener's first story was published in *Mirage*, he found himself inducted into a vibrant literary community and a lifelong friendship with Bellamy and Killian. "I think they're geniuses," he said when I asked about their relationship. "I think that Kevin's presence and support should not be overlooked. The stability of their relationship, and the tenderness, it's really significant."

Bellamy makes us tea, and we sit for another interview. Across the street from their bedroom, she points out, is the auto shop that for years released noxious fumes into the air, debilitating her for months and inciting "When the Sick Rule the World," the title essay of her most recent collection. In it Bellamy envisions a world centering the ill: "all perfume will be outlawed," she writes;[20] fragrant flowers will no longer be planted; "the sick will travel in packs commandeering porcelain-lined fragrance-free buses."[21] As the essay proceeds, it gets progressively, hilariously more outlandish: "When the sick rule the world the limbs of the well will be chopped off in the middle of the night."[22] In Bellamy's ambivalently flipped vision, the well are criminalized for pretending to be sick. I pop in another cough drop and ask her more about chronic illness.

"I got to where I was reacting to everything. I was sick all the time," she tells me. "Both my cats died of cancer." She speculates that her

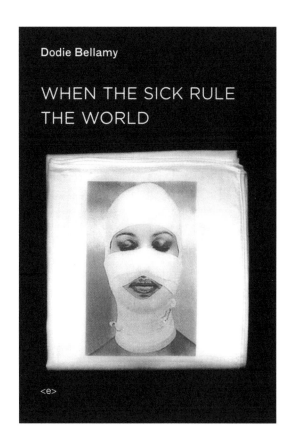

illness was related in some way to the laced marijuana from years earlier, which left her body more susceptible to chemical poisoning. She had previously gone to a nutritionist who advised her to cut out gluten, which helped with some sensitivities, but she "was getting worse and worse." She went to a naturopath who suggested chelation therapy, an alternative medicine practice that involves taking chemicals that bind to the metals in your bloodstream and removing them through urine—"it's supposed to be very difficult on people," Bellamy says. "There's no fucking way I could do that." The other option, of course, was to move, which wasn't really an option: it would mean leaving a rent-controlled apartment in an otherwise unaffordable city.

So she read up on environmental illness. "People die of this. It was amazing, their lives. I visited the safe house in Marin, and it was so horrifying, it really motivated me. I was going to do anything to get my shit together. I was not going to be one of those people." She got a powerful medical-grade HEPA air purifier, which helped to some extent. Then the body shop was sold, the fumes stopped, and her health improved.

Bellamy still has occasional drug flashbacks and other sensitivities, generally triggered by stress, and continues to do grounding exercises and other forms of energy work. Right now, she's in the middle of an online course on witch practices—that's where she got the Witch Camp shirt. "It's becoming a total cliché now," she says about witchcraft, "so that's horrible. But witchcraft is grounded in the earth, in the planets. It's very physical. You don't just sit there and think about things. It's all about moving energy through doing things through your body." She's enthusiastic explaining it, then swerves to distance herself. "I don't really tell people about it," she says, "because it's really stupid and embarrassing." Is it? I'm reminded of a passage in "Cultured," where Bellamy writes about spirituality as a form of low culture. "New Narrative Dodie versus New Age Dodie. Can one ever stop embarrassing the other? Dare I reclaim what's considered vulgar in spirituality?"[23] She sees my confusion. "I don't *really* care," she adds.

"Just passing through," says Killian cheerfully. He waves on his way to the bedroom, letting us talk.

She has similar ambivalence about her relationship to group therapy, specifically the eating disorder support group in Marin that she attended for five years, which helped her end a fifteen-year struggle with bulimia. "It was the dopiest thing that you could imagine," she tells me, "and it's the only time therapy's been useful for me." In "Beyond Hunger," she credits this support group with actually saving her life. "How do I write about something this profound without sounding sappy?" she wonders. "Maybe sappiness exists for a reason—for those situations where aesthetics are superfluous, where irony has no hold."[24] The wryness, the sardonic tone, is a distancing tactic, I'm learning, for someone who is deeply sensitive. (Boone: "It's a protective thing, her deadpan face. What can you read on that face? Nothing. Well, that's a defense strategy. But that doesn't mean there's not humor going on when you hear the sarcasm.")

We finish our tea, and Bellamy takes me on a walking tour of her SOMA neighborhood. We turn onto Eleventh Street, and she shows me where the body parts of a murdered man were discovered in 2015, a series of events chronicled in the coda to "In the Shadow of Twitter Towers," the closing essay of *When the Sick Rule the World*. A diaristic account of the months before and after the opening of the Twitter headquarters on Market Street in 2012, the essay traces a brief history of SOMA from old bohemia to the hippie era, to Bellamy's moving in during the era of punk and heroin, to this new moment of Twitter and Uber, meth and fentanyl. "A bad place doesn't spring up on its own," she writes. "Something creates it. Atrocity births ghosts; soulless gentrification herds the desperate into ghettos away from moneyed eyes of tourists."[25]

Bellamy walks rigidly, carrying herself carefully, a grim march. At the corner is the Firestone Tires where a leg was found in a trashcan. Across the street, where the Goodwill used to be, a human torso and leg were discovered in a suitcase. That corner is being decimated. The As Is store, where homeless people bought and sold clothes at a profit, has also been torn down to make way for a high-rise. It's a big hole now, giant, something surreally apocalyptic about its scale. We turn onto Market, and there it is: Twitter's world headquarters, marked by a vertical sign reading "@twitter" in gold. We enter The Market Café for lunch.

In the essay, Bellamy is astutely blasé about this new gentrification: she sees it all, a critically ambivalent documentarian. She includes a hypothetical letter to Twitter proposing a workshop: "Twitter is all about first personal narrative—my specialty. I can bring your employees to a new appreciation of the person. I can teach them how to connect tweets into longer narratives to counter the fragmentation inherent in the 140-character modality. As a long-time resident in your neighborhood, I can provide Twitter employees with an appreciation of our neighborhood's history, its rich cultural production and diversity."[26] The letter makes the case for the essay itself, which at nearly sixty pages offers an indispensable long view.

Bellamy assembles a meal from the salad and hot bars: greens, beets, quinoa, edamame, chickpeas, dressing. I order some five-dollar tea. We sit, then change seats so both of us can hear better. We're starting to grow exhausted. We try for an interview, but I'm having a hard time hearing, and the talking is keeping her from enjoying her salad. We cut it short. I head to a café to finish re-reading *the buddhist*, where I get cruised by a bearded man reading *The Secrets of People Who Never Get Sick*. He assumes I'm reading about Buddhism, has never heard of Dodie Bellamy, is confused when I explain the book is a series of confessional blog posts about a toxic relationship with a Buddhist spiritual leader. I could ask him how not to get sick but . . . I blow my nose pointedly. When I bring up *the buddhist* with Bellamy later, she highlights the community that formed around her blog as she was writing it, the kind of community that seems improbable in today's online spaces. "The peer policing that goes on now is like the opposite of the openness that produced *the buddhist*," she says. She sees her blog now as "another of these pockets of being connected to a broader community"—not unlike New Narrative. "Then it just dissolves."

The walls of the Wattis Bar are lined with blowups of the covers of Bellamy's books. The atmosphere is convivial, alive with bright chatter. Tonight's event is a series of readings by Bellamy's former students. Linda Bakke's piece about being burned as a child is vulnerable, intimate, painful with visceral details. Michele Carlson reads an engaging, tightly crafted text about the racial politics of her experience at an artists' commune. Carlos Jackson shares a piece with idiosyncratic and matter-of-fact sex scenes. I can hear Bellamy's influence.

Afterward we take a few cars to Saap Ver for dinner. I feel awful. My head hurts. It's terribly loud in the restaurant, which is broadcasting sports on large-screen TVs. I sneak another ibuprofen and, at Bellamy's recommendation, order the lemongrass soup, then wait passively for it to show up. Bellamy prods me: "You should talk to people." Right. I pull out my notebook and ask about her private living-room workshop, which most of these people have been part of.

"It's pretty famous," says Anne McGuire. "A famous underground thing." Bellamy started it before she pursued teaching college, in the late 1980s or early 1990s. "I had this therapist who told me to do it," Bellamy says. "It's something I never would have thought of doing. She basically modeled middle-class behavior for me."

The workshop initially ran three times a year; now it's just once in the summer. Among the other writers who have gone through it: novelist Andrea Lawlor, visual artist and writer Anne Walsh, writer Drew Cushing. "It's mostly people who want to write in this expansive personal way," says Bellamy.

"It's not super professional," says Carlson. "I really like the genrelessness."

Victoria Gannon comments on the community. "It's this gathering of people I can relate to. Most of us are writing in the arts."

Bellamy leans in. "Almost everyone's an artist." This isn't surprising— Bellamy has published a lot of writing on artists, from Raymond Pettibon (with whom she has collaborated), to Tariq Alvi, to, most recently, a feature on Mary Beth Edelson in *Artforum*, where she is also a regular columnist. "There are a certain group of writers that artists tend to like," said Viegener, who teaches at California Institute of the Arts. "Dodie is one of those. I think there's something about the conceptual insight and play behind her work. It has a self-consciousness plus a very sophisticated sense of language."

"Dodie writes brilliantly about artists," said Kraus. "She gets inside the head of the maker in a way that very few people do. She really understands the artist's process, and she's very generous in her descriptions of it. She is just kind of a genius at giving a shape and words to what a visual artist is actually doing."

Bakke's further down the table, and it's too loud to crosstalk so we step outside. Her first encounter with Bellamy was in her Writing on the Body class at SFSU, where Bellamy is a lecturer. "She is amazing," Bakke says. "I couldn't believe the work she was teaching." Bakke signed up for a class with her every semester from then on and eventually became her graduate instructional aide. An avid champion of Bellamy, she objects to what she sees as the department's underappreciation of Bellamy. "Every time I filled out course evals, I would say, 'You don't know what you're doing. You have a *treasure*.' I just think she's one of the greatest artists ever."

Cage's relationship with Bellamy tracks along similar lines: assistant, student, workshop participant, now good friend. She remembers her SFSU courses being life changing. "She was like the pied piper of queer and interesting writers. It was just this amazing array of students who were so thrilled and thriving on the writing she was assigning." Later she would take Dodie's summer workshops, which she describes as fun and intimate.

Beyond SFSU and CCA, Bellamy has held a number of other institutional teaching gigs over the years, including in the low-residency program at Antioch College, where Brooklyn-based writer Jeanne Thornton was her student in 2005. "I remember being really excited to work with her," Thornton told me in an email. "She was this cool experimental lesbian writer who seemed smart and remote and challenging. There was some manifest queerness in her work that I felt a really powerful pull from." Thornton was in the process of coming into a trans identity and found Bellamy's presence steadying and supportive. "It was very, very important."

"I think she's the Hans Hofmann of a kind of queer avant-garde prose writing," said Myles, referring to the artist whose unofficial school of painting spawned Abstract Expressionism in the years after World War II. "I mean, she's *such* a teacher. And like many great teachers, I think she's never had a secure teaching job. People bemoan shit like that, but it's good news. The thing that's funny about teaching wildly is that it's the most passionate kind of teaching; it's the most influential. It's really a great thing, though I'm sure it hasn't always felt that way. She's probably the great feminist art-writing teacher of her generation."

"Do you feel secure financially?" I ask Bellamy later. She responds, "Not at all." When adjuncts rule the world, I think, provosts will inherit our debt. The tenured will take over our course loads as we take over their full-salaried sabbaticals. "I'll probably be one of those people who have one of those Facebook fundraisers," she goes on, laughing. "'Keep her off the street.'"

When I return to the Bay Area five months later for a writing retreat, I'm hoping for a redo—some time with Bellamy when I'm not clouded

with congestion and cold medicine. She's game and offers to set up
a class visit so I can get paid: adjunct solidarity. The class, focused
on gender and literature, is dynamic and energized, and it's hard
to reconcile her success as a teacher with her precarious status as
an adjunct. We talk a bit about my work—she's assigned "Slug,"
an erotic fantasy that I wrote channeling Dodie Bellamy years ago,
probably my favorite of the stories I've written. Discussion is lively. I
want to impart to these young people, who probably don't know, how
monumental Bellamy is, how groundbreaking her work is, but I don't
think I can shift into that gear without making things awkward for all
of us. I refrain.

How does one talk—how does one write—about someone whose
impact has been so profound without sounding sappy? I don't know.
In their letters and cards to one another, Kevin and Dodie are sappy
all the time. Big saps. "I love you I love you I love you!" swoons one
Post-it from Dodie to Kevin. "Dear Kins," reads a gallant anniversary
card message from Kevin to Dodie, "Was it 15 years or 15 minutes?
Love you madly." When I get home, I interview Myles and Kraus and
send Dodie some select quotes. She forwards them to Kevin, who
sends over a collection of tributes from other writers in celebration
of her sixty-fifth birthday. "They may amuse you, my dear Megan,"
he writes. "I don't mean to lard up your piece with all this stuff,
but they may give you some further leads, right?" The list brings
together mentors like Glück ("you have changed so many lives");
peers like Dennis Cooper ("Dodie is probably the genius writer of my
generation"); and younger writers like Wendy C. Ortiz ("Dodie, your
name has been whispered & thought repeatedly in my house because
you are one of my favorite writers") and Maggie Nelson ("Dodie is an
inspiration, a provocation, a legend, a treasure, and a call to arms").
Kevin is right: I'm amused and touched. I want to cosign all of it.

Better yet, a spell. When I rule the world, Dodie Bellamy will win
the MacArthur "Genius Grant." She will have won it years ago, had
her pick of cushy teaching jobs lathering her up in more money and
recognition, more time. When *Cunt-Ups* is re-released, it will win
seventeen National Book Awards, one for each year it's won none,
with a few Guggenheims for good measure, plus a long list of other
prizes I can't remember because I, too, try to avoid giving them
much sway. When I rule the world, those crude geniuses like Dodie,
the weird, working-class women who aren't "prizes and awards type
writer[s]," will win them all, and ruling the world, they'll get read,
they'll get recognized, they'll get paid. Dodie-style, I could probably
go more audacious here, think big, change everything: not just
aesthetic elitism but classism and ageism at large, not to mention
white supremacist heteropatriarchy, late capitalism, the world. At
the end of "In the Shadow of Twitter Towers," Bellamy describes
an "urban witch" in her alley, holding a branch upright like a wand.
She taps once, taps twice on Eleventh Street, and the world, Dodie
imagines, corrects itself. Tap, tap, on my keyboard. I'm moving the
energy. I'm making change.

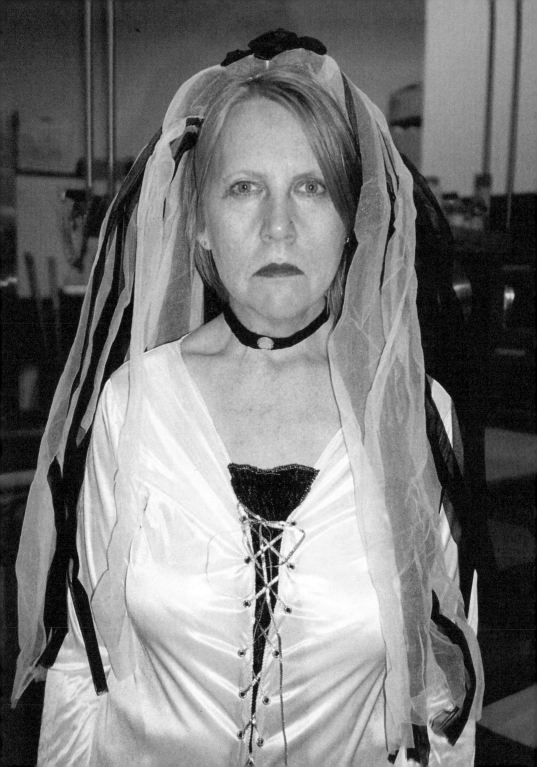

Tiny Revolts

by ANDREW DURBIN

The following essay was first delivered as a lecture at the CCA Wattis Institute on September 20, 2018.

1.

I n 1989, the British filmmaker Derek Jarman, then living in a seaside cottage near the nuclear power plant in Dungeness, England, complained in his diary of "the terrible dearth of information, the fictionalization of our experience" in contemporary queer writing. "Why novelize it when the best of it is in our lives?" Jarman voiced a familiar lament, one that sees fiction as engaged in an impossible competition with reality that it cannot but lose. The context for his objection was the destruction of the queer community by AIDS, a time in which "all the best and brightest were trampled to death." He likened the crisis to what it must have felt like to face the mounting losses of friends and lovers, family and colleagues during the First World War. It seemed to him that anything but an art of the real was not up to the task of addressing all those who were then "dying for love."[1]

Around this time, in San Francisco, Dodie Bellamy lectured on autobiography at Small Press Distribution, a nonprofit literary organization now based in Berkeley. Without knowing of Jarman's criticism of contemporary writing, since it had yet to find its way to publication, but with this same conflict between fiction and autobiography in mind, she made an argument, in a lecture titled "Incarnation," for a literature that sees the two as interrelated and possessing complementary strategies for constructing first-person narratives. And more importantly, for a writing with nerve, feeling, and sex: "a writing that can know pus as come," as she writes in *Cunt-Ups*, her 2001 collection of "21 pornographic chapters."[2] It is also a writing with politics, a writing that doesn't shirk its responsibilities to a complex world; a writing that sees both information and fictionalization as integral to the representation of the best, or at least the most interesting aspects, of our lives.

"In the contest of 'Imagination vs. Reality,'" she announced to her audience, "I am drawn to 'versus.'"[3] Bellamy's rejection of binary thinking (and its replacement with hybridity, that "versus") is a hallmark of New Narrative—the loosely defined cohort of poets and novelists to which Bellamy has been aligned since the 1980s, many of whom lived in the Bay Area. Working from the late 1970s onward, the writers associated with the movement prioritized transparency in order to make clear the compositional and political strategies that define a text and its speaker, whom the reader is often meant to take for (some version of) the author. In their introduction to *Writers Who Love Too Much* (2017), an anthology of New Narrative writing edited by Bellamy and her late partner Kevin Killian, they note that this Bay Area–based avant-garde

> responded to post-structuralist quarrels with traditional
> storytelling practice for inscribing "master narrative," and
> attempted to open up the field to a wider range of subjects

and subject positions. It would be a writing prompted not by
fiat nor consensus, nor by the totalizing suggestions of the
MFA "program era," but by community; it would be unafraid
of experiment, unafraid of kitsch, unafraid of sex and gossip
and political debate.[4]

While New Narrative wasn't born out of the AIDS crisis, it did
respond directly to its concerns and to the experiences of men and
women living with the disease through a direct address of sex and
the body. Arguably, the failure of the government to respond to
that crisis, which was spreading throughout the artistic and literary
communities in New York and San Francisco, provided the movement
with a sense of urgency as it attempted to deconstruct and contradict
prevailing—and normalizing—trends in literature that often excluded
or downplayed queer lives.

Part of this urgency draws from the fact that some of its key members
died of AIDS at exactly the moment when they were producing their
major works and expanding their audience. This included Steve
Abbott and Sam D'Allesandro, with whom Bellamy exchanged a
number of letters collected in her book *Real: The Letters of Mina
Harker and Sam D'Allesandro* (1994). But rather than mope or simply
mourn or bid farewell in lush symphonies composed of harmonies for
a slipping world; rather than retreat into fearful, anxious literature;
rather than deny, obfuscate, or look elsewhere, away from the body,
away from its vulnerabilities, New Narrative looked inward (and
forward)—not only at the author, but at the author's body, with
its weaknesses, its susceptibilities, its liability to change and feel
pleasure, to live and to die, and found there not only a self, but *a self
among selves*, a self constituted by—and constituent of—a community.
And this remains one of the movement's greatest lessons, one that

runs contrary to the impulses of many contemporary mainstream novelists, who so often silo their books in a first-person narrative of glittering, romantic cliché—or, as Dennis Cooper put it in "Purplish Prose," his 1994 essay on the so-called Violet Quill novelists whose work, in many ways, serves as a precursor to today's popular but often conservative queer writing, in which "likeable gay characters dealt likeably with traditional everyday traumas."[5] Not New Narrative, into which Cooper is sometimes corralled.

New Narrative, as one of its founding members Robert Glück wrote, is a "hybrid aesthetic" that names names and strips itself bare before the reader, transforming the book "into a social practice that is lived."[6] It is a writing built out of a play with the construction of scene and character, and with the assumptions typically made by the reader herself. For example, does this "I" belong to the woman writing the book? Or, as another poet once put it, is she "a complex of occasions"—built of words, sentences, scenes, ideas, analysis, and introspection not coincident with reality but emerging *from* it to posit a new "I" entirely, one for whom reality—the apparently nonfictional, confessional element of writing—is only a starting point.

"An illusion of confession is purposely created," Bellamy argues in "Incarnation." "It's superfluous whether or not the content is 'true.' The 'autobiographical' first person is now about tone, a technique for creating intimacy, sometimes discomfort, in the reader."[7]

"Intimacy" and "sometimes discomfort" are two aspects of Bellamy's writing that I want to discuss in this lecture and, in particular, the ways they complement one another. Neither tone or mode is distinct from one another, nor are they always the essential qualities in Bellamy's work, but often enough they are—and when they are, they act in concert, or at least through linkages that build, then break, build and break. They are two shifting, bounded undercurrents to her writing that carry us through the text. In 2011's *the buddhist*, Bellamy's account of an affair with a yogi that originated on her blog, *Belladodie*, she moves between the despairing frustrations and futility that attend to love and writing, and also the release provided by our friends and lovers, our kin and fellow "hydra-heads" (to whom the book is dedicated): "Seize tenderness by the balls,"[8] she writes. In Bellamy's work, spheres of discomfort and intimacy widen and narrow telescopically through her insuperable "I," which is only, after all, a technique. But it is a technique designed to constantly expand the first person beyond biography or lived experience toward emergent and hypothetical politics, theories, ideas, and, importantly, relations that do not yet exist in the real world but must be imagined anyway. As she writes in her 2006 collection of essays, *Academonia*, writing "has always been a way to worm my way back into . . . freedom, that incendiary in-between state, to court anxiety, instability, glorious fuckedupness."[9]

In "Incarnation," she quotes her high school diary, citing a passage that offers a cogent thesis for her work overall: "In the grandiose style of a sixteen year old I wrote, 'The three things which interest me most in the world are sex, death and literature.' Things haven't changed much in the past 20 years except that lately I've been drawn to the subtler aspects of life, the way the numinous peeks through the daily."[10]

2.

November 2011: Crummy video shows protestors flinging themselves against the police on the UC Berkeley campus, where students and professors march against economic and racial injustice roiling the campus. We see cops fan out on the lawn, armed with pepper spray and batons. They drag professors across the grass by their hair, disperse crowds with smoke bombs, beat kids begging for help for their injured peers. You must remember, as I remember, the photograph of UC Davis students sitting on the sidewalk, their hands zip-tied behind their backs, while a cop sprays them with an orange blast of chemicals: one of the most striking images of the past decade and one that resonated around the world for weeks.

In "The Beating of Our Hearts," Bellamy's 2012 essay on the democratic relations that were established, if briefly, during and around the Occupy movement in Oakland, Bellamy considers the ways propaganda—specifically, an ad for Barack Obama's reelection campaign—and images of protest, including those on university campuses, prompt an inner alertness to political mindfulness, a sense that we are not simply alone, after all, but alone with others, struggling against the concatenating violence of an overly parental state.[11] "The commitment to radicalism," she writes, "like a religious conversion, is not arrived at logically. It is caught—through a gesture, an image that strikes us to our core." This struggle, which takes place between bodies, is almost always tinged with the erotic, Bellamy notes. She finds the Occupy poets who were active at this time "hot," and they are; this sexiness she links, as she often links sexiness, to a historical continuum of like-minded bodies engaged in allied struggle—to protestors before these UC students, like the marchers during the Civil Rights movement of the 1960s, when Bellamy was in high school and watched the nightly news in her parents' living room in Indiana. They are "marvelously intense," she writes.

The essay blends reportage with analysis of the work of other writers, the effects of a film's speed on our understanding of our recorded

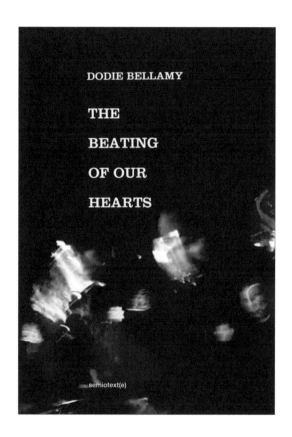

experience, and the ways "connection hails us when least expected"
to address the *jetztzeit*—Benjaminian now-time—of collective action
and awareness. "The protest poster is . . . an intimate gesture,"
she writes. It "reaches beyond our intellectual understanding, our
sophistication, and sidles up to our vulnerability: people are hurting,
bad things are being done." In the essay, she reads at a house in
Berkeley, an event that devolves, as readings like it must, into a dance
party. Someone puts on the original 45 of the Tommy James and the
Shondells' song, "I Think We're Alone Now," and the poets dance all
evening, a scene Bellamy finds deeply moving. Only days before, they
were being "thwacked in the ribs with billy clubs." She considers the
song playing on the stereo, the way "we" can be alone together as
"revolutionaries on the run."[12] It begins:

> *Children behave, that's what they say when we're together*
> *And watch how you play*
> *They don't understand*
> *And so we're*
>
> *Running just as fast as we can, holdin' on to one another's hands*
> *Tryin' to get away into the night and then you put your arms around me*
> *And we tumble to the ground and then you say*
>
> *I think we're alone now*
> *There doesn't seem to be anyone around*
> *I think we're alone now*
> *The beating of our hearts is the only sound*

The song, she writes, "can easily be reclaimed as an anthem for
[those] revolutionaries on the run." And Bellamy sees here, in the
poets dancing to the song, a larger metaphor: here is a politics, here

is a struggle, and here also, finally, are moments of relative peace, one brokered within the realm of political and economic violence, and inextricably linked to it.

"I felt profoundly alive," she writes. And this, for me, is a quintessential moment in Bellamy's writing: islands of the personal upon which we, the reader, land in order to come to terms with Bellamy's roving critique of sex, power, gender, poetry, and identity. The "fictionalization of our experience," to return to Jarman's phrase, does not necessarily mean a novelist (or essayist interested in fiction) reneges on her responsibility to address her place in the world or the world itself; rather it allows for an expanded understanding of that place as *a place among places*, just as it does a *self among selves*. A house in Berkeley is not a house; it is a symbol resonant with all houses like it, that "marvelously intense" opposition arrayed across time and geography.

Why novelize it, as Jarman says, when the best—these houses, these dance parties—is in our lives? We might say that, often enough, the "best" lives outside ourselves and cannot be reached except through imagination (how else to place a house party in Berkeley in relation to protest of the twentieth century) and novelization—a term that I define loosely to mean the conversion of events into a story, whether it be "fiction" or "nonfiction." For me, the "or" between genres might be named as a third category, and one to which Bellamy's work broadly seems to belong. That is, the category of "experimental fiction," that inter- or even contra-genre writing of "immediacy," to borrow a term from Kathy Acker, who has been an important touchstone in Bellamy's work. Acker wrote, in a 1990 essay on Jean Genet and William S. Burroughs, about "the other tradition" to which they, as well as Acker and Bellamy, belong: "'Marginal,' 'experimental,' and

BARF
manifesto

dodie bellamy

'avant-garde' are often words used to describe texts in this other tradition," she writes. "Not because [such writing] is marginal, but because our society, through the voice of its literary society, cannot bear immediacy, the truth, especially the political truth."[13]

3.

I first read Bellamy when a boyfriend gave me a copy of *Barf Manifesto*. We were at a party in some green precinct of Brooklyn. It might have been a birthday for a poet. A few people were dancing to pop hits from the period. I stood with my boyfriend near the bookshelves, our fingers scanning the spines of poetry collections as we searched for something to read aloud in honor of the friend we were celebrating. Our search led nowhere. Everyone was too busy surreptitiously bumping coke in the bathroom and dancing to the booming pop of the time for poetry to matter, or at least to matter in that charged moment. Perhaps one illustrative difference between the poetry scenes of the Bay Area and New York is that, in New York, we would have plugged in an iPod and played Rihanna's "You Da One" rather than the blowsy pop of the 1960s. My own essay from this moment might have been called "You Da One," and rather than dwell on the way Rihanna's own liberating poetics might be extended to our lives, *My love is your love, your love is mine*, I would write about *Barf Manifesto*, a copy of which we found in a pile of chapbooks on the coffee table. My boyfriend, who had read it before, handed it to me with the advice, "I'd steal this because you're not going to want to let it go once you read it." He then left for the bathroom, drawn into the dark by the shine of an apartment key laced with cocaine.

I smuggled the chapbook out of the party and spent the next morning reading though a hangover. The essay is divided into two parts and concerns a short essay by Eileen Myles called "Everyday Barf" and Bellamy's friendship with her. She opens with a close reading of Myles's piece, which recounts the poet's disagreement with an editor who commissioned her to write a sestina. In Myles's essay, her editor deems her attempt at the form insufficient. Fuck form, she writes. She concludes with a scene on the Provincetown ferry as a storm comes in, melancholic that she couldn't convince her eighty-three-year-old mother to return to the mainland with her.[14] Bellamy writes that Myles's essay, and let's say from the outset here that the passage I'm about to quote applies to all of Bellamy's own writing and that's why I'm bringing it up, "argues against essentialism, generalizing, pinning things down, forcing experience into predetermined form. It is a manifesto"—a body of work—"of complexity, ambiguity, indeterminacy, layering, contradiction, blurring of boundaries, in which Myles [and, again, let's say Bellamy] tracks how the personal intersects content intersects form intersects politics."[15]

Bellamy introduces a number of hallmarks of her work in her reading of "Everyday Barf," from an analysis of genre—the essay, which she's "always found oppressive, a form so conservative it begs to be dismantled"—to a series of anecdotes about art, friendship, and teaching. She worries about workplace jealousies and reports of a holly cure that she might try to remedy her feelings. She sees, in Chicago, Grant Wood's painting *American Gothic* (1930) while visiting the city for the Modern Language Association conference, which had prompted her to write the second half of *Barf Manifesto*.

There is one key scene for me, however, that bears reading in full. In 2006, Bellamy visited Myles in San Diego, where the poet was then teaching:

. . . when I arrive at Eileen's house it's late and there's no
toilet paper, so Eileen brings in a roll of paper towels from
the kitchen, this'll have to do, she says. I tear off a sheet, then
rip that in half, trying to use the smallest piece possible but
the next morning when I have a bowel movement it won't go
down, the toilet water fills to the brim, precariously quivering,
then Eileen's handing me a plunger and telling me to pump
and to keep pumping until all the water is gone, it's first thing
in the morning and I haven't had coffee, and it's hot as hell,
I'm wearing this thin white organic cotton nightgown, with
peach and white embroidered vines on it, and I'm sweating
as I pump my breasts are bobbing crazily for all the world to
see, the water finally goes down and I flush and the toilet fills
up again with my horrible smelly poo, my shame, and Eileen's
in the doorway barking, keep pumping, pump until all the
water's gone, and I argue that's not going to work and Eileen
argues that's what she did in New York, and I'm flopping
about and sweating and pumping, on the wall beside me hangs
the black and white Mapplethorpe photo of a young Eileen,
it's such a bright morning, keep pumping Eileen barks and
I'm feeling like this miserable worm, I want to shout it's not
my fault, but it is my fault, my crap clogged her plumbing
and she's showing no mercy, outside grow all those weird
tropical plants imported from Hawaii, I took some photos of
Eileen in tank top and shorts watering them, John Granger,
who teaches nature writing told me that the landscape of
San Diego is all fake, some rich woman at some point liked
the look of Hawaii and that was that, I doubt John used the
work fake, fake is my word for sure, the way my mom called
nonindigenous plants "foreign plants," she said it with a
scowl, "those foreign plants," which so perfectly sums up the

conservative Midwestern America I grew up in, for hours
I watched my mother gasp then jerk her head to the left,
each breath was like this big event, gasp jerk pause gasp jerk
pause and the nurses assured me this was a peaceful cancer
death and I believed them—gasping and jerking my mother
was at peace—I had to believe them. The last time I taught
"Everyday Barf," a paralyzed woman in a wheelchair said
people don't want to think about the body because it reminds
them of their vulnerability, the woman breathes through a tube
that she closes her lips around like a straw. So I'm pumping,
pumping but the water's going down way too slowly, my crap's
all wrong, too much for Eileen's plumbing, I'm begging her
this isn't working, jiggling breasts, pump she says, that same
trip her ancient pitbull Rosie pissed on the dining room floor,
and Eileen cleaned it up so tenderly, petting Rosie, telling her
it was alright, and I hate that she's treating me worse than a
dog. The vulnerable body subverts the forward propulsion of
the narrative arc, that fantasy of progress, resolution. As Julia
Kristeva posits in *Powers of Horror*, bodily emissions point up
our morality, our impending thingness.[16]

In her essay "Crimes Against Genre," included in *Academonia*,
Bellamy quotes the anthropologist Mary Douglas, who defines the
unclean as "matter out of place . . . that which must not be included
if a pattern is to be maintained." Douglas cites monstrous births as
an example, and Bellamy builds on Douglas to argue that we might
see experimental writing itself as monstrous, as that which refuses
pattern and therefore is itself unclean: a turd, barf. Excrement—and
refuse—has long been a favored metaphor for critics dismissive
of quote unquote bad writing, experimental writing, writing that
dispenses with genre. "What shit," some critic might write. We

use it ourselves all the time. When we dislike a film, find its plot or mise-en-scène unsuitable to our taste, we tell our friends, "Oh, it was garbage." Someone we disagree with is full of "crap," too. Some books are "trash." He "laid a turd" with his newest album. That play was "total bullshit."

Sometimes these expressions of disapproval can make a work seem appealing, its badness intriguing. "It's so bad you have to see it," for example. Experimental, or queer, writing—and art in general— has long sought to recuperate trash, shit, garbage, and to find in the rejected a poetics of recycled, regurgitated, and therefore new forms. (A revolutionary undoing.) John Waters, the famous pope of trash, had Divine eat dog shit in *Pink Flamingos*. It might be a deliberately provocative scene meant to disgust us, but it is precisely this affirmation of *being* disgusting that frees her, on-screen, to be something totally, thrillingly new.

The turd scene in *Barf Manifesto* made a significant impression on me. I had never read anything like it: for one, while there are numerous scenes of defecation in literature, they are mostly private, often funny (see Shakespeare) and mostly told by men—and each is remarkably different than Dodie's episode for its explicit humiliation (rather than release). James Joyce, in *Ulysses*: "Quietly he read, restraining himself, the first column and, yielding but resisting, began the second. Midway, his last resistance yielding, he allowed his bowels to ease themselves quietly as he read, reading still patiently, that slight constipation of yesterday quite gone." Karl Ove Knausgaard's *My Struggle* deals extensively with shitting, and he even wrote an as yet untranslated essay about defecation, "The Brown Tail." Interestingly, though, Bellamy uses the toilet to introduce the image of her dying mother, recalling a much older poetic model, one originally found in

Chaucer, who sometimes used stool, defecation, etc., to disrupt genre modes, as Susan Signe Morrison notes in an essay on "fecopoetics." She writes of *The Reeve's Tale*:

> Filth does not just belong to the fabliau; it is everywhere human actors are present. Alison's "hol," punctuated by Nicholas's fart, destroys Absolon's courtly love fantasy. The Reeve attempts to control the danger or phantom of sexual assault through genre manipulation. The genre of the poignant dawn song spoken between Malyne and Aleyn interrupts the ostensible fabliau of *The Reeve's Tale*, exposing this romantic encounter as rape. By forcing a disjunction of genres, signaled through excrement (when Symken's wife goes to piss), Chaucer discomforts us. Chaucer allows the disjunction, this rupture of the fabliau, to alert the reader to the problem of functioning solely within a genre. We want to passively succumb to the genre; we desire the oppression genres wield through their own version of social control. But Chaucer does not let us wallow in our generic ease.[17]

Likewise, Bellamy does not allow us to stay long in the toilet and uses the broken plumbing to break the scene's concentration and move us out of the house, to the imported plants of San Diego, all the way to Indiana, to Bellamy's dying mother. We understand, in Bellamy's use of Kristeva, that we are meant to see this unsinkable turd as not merely what it is, but as a totem, too, one that links Bellamy—and Myles, who was attending to the dying Rosie (that story is now the subject of Myles's 2017 book *Afterglow*)—to their mortality. It is itself a body, disintegrating in the water, without a place to go, and in this, I see an image for the transformative potential of writing, too, one that converts humiliation to tenderness and back again.

Putting the turd in *Barf Manifesto* is much like putting the dog shit in *Pink Flamingos*. Its presence is not meant only to prompt our disgust, though it might do that, too, but rather to call our attention to those breakages in literary decorum and expectation, those patterns that dominate normative writing, through the jarring presence of this dark metonym for the text itself; it "subverts the forward propulsion of the narrative arc" and in doing so suspends us over the toilet of the text, in which we might glimpse, as the piece's title promises, a manifesto—that which is made obvious, that which erupts from the bowl, which cannot be flushed and floods the floor. It doesn't simply shock; rather it produces discomfort, which is uglier and more powerful than shock. It makes you squirm. In this, Bellamy theorizes refuse (barf, shit, snot, pus, mucus, come) as a "literary form," and perhaps the preeminent form of our era of ejecta and the one to which we might champion her as its founder:

> The Barf is feminist, unruly, cheerfully monstrous. The Barf comes naturally to women because women like to throw up *fingers down throat, one, two, three, bleh. . . .* The Barf is an upheaval, born of our hangover from imbibing too much Western Civ. The Barf is reflective, each delivery calls forth a framing, the Barf is expansive as the Blob, swallowing and recontextualizing, spreading out and engorging. Its logic is associative, it proceeds by chords rather than single, discrete notes. Hierarches jumble in the thrill, in the imperatives of purge.[18]

Or, to return to an earlier phrase, the imperatives of "the peeking numinous." It is an imperative—barf—that gives Bellamy's work an absorptive framework through which all might find its belonging, its connection. It's the stinging of bile as it rises in your throat only to

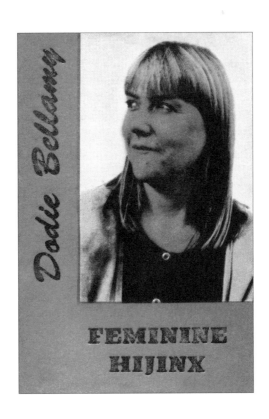

Dodie Bellamy

FEMININE HIJINX

spill out from your mouth into the bowl, your shirt, your lap. The hood of a car, a back alley. It is also a framework that allows Bellamy to constantly rewrite the terms of her engagement with the world, as a woman, as a writer, as a reader; it's a mixing within, followed by expulsion. Barf is everything, barf is history, barf is present, barf is future: barf is love, barf is form, and it is formlessness. It is intimacy; it is sometimes discomfort—and between these form an I.

4.

I wrote the ending of this lecture several times. There are so many directions available in thinking about Dodie—and here, finally, I want to use her first name, since she's not just a writer who's been important to me as a reader over the years, she's also been a friend, someone whose voice I turn to not only on the page, but in email, on the phone, at dinner, and so on. I could continue to look at essays, poems. There's the opening of the *TV Sutras*, for example, which Dodie wrote while meditating in front of her TV. There's her first book, *Feminine Hijinx*, which fits in your palm. I could even have written about her incomplete manuscripts, those projects I've only heard rumors of. There's so much I missed.

But in my notes from the start, I had two words and a name typed at the end of this document: "Boyfriend, tenderness." I've forgotten what I meant by them. Perhaps I had wanted to write that boyfriend back into the story, though I'm not sure how I would have done so since I made him up. In truth, I found Dodie's work at that birthday party on my own. I invented a lover to make a point about the alliance of readers who surround this work, who promote it—you know, that lovers give each other copies of Dodie Bellamy's work, and isn't that remarkable? What was the point of that? Once I put him in, I couldn't excise him from the final version, even for this publication.

There's something to be said about made-up love. We invent it all the time in our work—these relations, these characters, these stories, these essays of the best of our lives. Sometimes they condense multiple men and women into one, and sometimes they're simply those whom we wish we had had in our lives but didn't. That's what makes writing so great. Or what makes queer writing so great—that invention, contrivance; the fictionalization of our lives allows us to rewrite the world to suit our needs, and I suppose so long as it's done with an ethics in mind and with a sense of the responsibilities of the imagination, it might be an antidote to our decade replete with so much public lying. Perhaps that's too vague a claim—I'm not sure I've worked it out yet. What's true is that I stole the chapbook without anyone's recommendation, and so, oddly enough, I first encountered her work by theft. It was a tender theft. A different kind of love: a self-love. That must have been why I wrote tenderness, too.

Reading Dodie Bellamy: Vulnerability and Vulgarity

by KAYE MITCHELL

I n *Carnal Appetites* (2000), Elspeth Probyn addresses "questions
of appetite, of excess, of fear, shame and disgust," arguing
that, "by bringing the dynamics of shame and disgust into
prominence we are forced to envision a more visceral and powerful
corporeal politics."[1] The relationship that she proceeds to posit
between disgust and shame is, in my opinion, too schematic, and
her definition of both too narrow,[2] but in Probyn's recognition
of "the way in which disgust and shame may illumine the body's
capacities for reaching out and spilling across domains that we
would like to keep separate, or hidden from view," she offers a useful
starting point for reading the work of Dodie Bellamy.[3] As a novelist,
poet, and essayist emerging from the alternative literary scene in
San Francisco, associated since the 1980s with the New Narrative
movement, Bellamy has produced a body of work that thwarts genre
boundaries and, in her own words, "[champions] the vulnerable, the
fractured, the disenfranchised, the fucked-up."[4] Probyn's "spilling
out" arguably expresses both the content and the form of much of
Bellamy's work: from its confessional and sexually explicit elements,
to its use of appropriation from apparently culturally discrete sources
such as canonical poetry, high theory, pop culture, and pornography.
Bellamy pursues this "unguarded embrace of cultural artifacts,"

while eschewing what she calls "the mainstream avant-garde's condescension towards pop culture—using it as a source of parody that the author remains intellectually and morally superior to." Instead, she refuses that distance, that superiority, claiming that "a more honest and interesting approach to pop culture is to delight in its tackiness but at the same time admit you're profoundly moved by it."[5] The "profound" and the "tacky" are thereby positioned as not mutually exclusive; "unguarded," meanwhile, expresses remarkably precisely both the method (scattershot) and the feeling (vulnerable, unprotected) of this "embrace of cultural artifacts."

Significantly, Bellamy also connects this (fascination with) "lowness" to femaleness, asserting that "[a]ggressively female experience and the female body are still denigrated by the avant-garde, and thus, to write from the position of one's femaleness is still to commit oneself to low culture."[6] In this essay, I argue that such modes and methods allow Bellamy to tread a line between vulnerability and vulgarity in a manner that exemplifies the double-functioning of shame, particularly for the writer who "write[s] from the position of [her] femaleness": that is to say, shame functions both as constitutive and as critical of femininity; it invokes and involves both a desire for spectacle and a desire for self-concealment; as Silvan Tomkins writes, "In shame I wish to continue to look and be looked at, but I also do not wish to do so."[7] Bellamy's work, I suggest, is not simply or straightforwardly *shameless*, because it demonstrates a keen awareness of, and commitment to, a certain "low culture" of female embodiment and a degraded "feminine" culture of the mainstream and the "tacky"; its relationship to shame is not, therefore, one of redemption or overcoming but rather something more immersive, complex, and complicitous, which produces more dissonant effects both formally and politically.

Such an understanding of shame—and its relationship to femininity—
both builds on and complicates that posited by Sandra Bartky in
Femininity and Domination (1990), wherein she argues that, "It is
in the act of being shamed and in the feeling ashamed that there is
disclosed to women who they are and how they are faring within the
domains they inhabit."[8] Bartky asserts that shame is "gender-related"
in the sense that "women are more prone to experience" shame
than men, and because "the feeling itself has a different meaning in
relation to their total psychic situation and general social location
than has a similar emotion when experienced by men."[9] Shame,
then, experienced as or through "a pervasive sense of personal
inadequacy" and as or through "the shame of embodiment," reveals
"the 'generalized condition of dishonour' that is women's lot in sexist
society."[10] For women, feelings of shame "are profoundly disclosive
of [their] 'Being-in-the-world.'"[11] The simultaneously structural
and personal nature of shame for women is certainly something
that Bellamy's work explores and exemplifies; however, the question
that inaugurates this essay is what is altered in this experience of
shame—and disclosure of self—when the "act of being shamed" is
instead an act of self-shaming, an embrace of a shamed position or
an apparently shameless appropriation of material that may itself be
shameful; all of these practices are found in Bellamy's work and/or
form part of her writing philosophy. What forms of self-disclosure-
through-shame are thereby made possible? What relationships are
instantiated between shame and femininity, shame and writing in the
"exultation in lowness" that is Bellamy's writing?[12] To what extent
might we read this phrase—"exultation in lowness"—as a distinctly
gendered expression of what, for Giorgio Agamben, forms part of the
definitive experience of shame (and, indeed, of "the fundamental
sentiment of being a *subject*"): "to be *subjected* and to be *sovereign*"?[13]
Arguably, gendered embodiment, for Bellamy, is indissociable from

her writing practice and is the locus of her experiences of both subjection and sovereignty.

The apparently shameless and transgressive elements of Bellamy's writing have been frequently noted. Bellamy's work might be read as "transgressive" in the sense discussed by Peter Stallybrass and Allon White in *The Politics and Poetics of Transgression*, because of the extent to which it allows the "low" or "base" to trouble the "high" or "exalted," thereby challenging the most fundamental "mechanisms of ordering and sense-making" in Western cultures and producing, in turn, a deliberate disorder at the level of the page.[14] However, while Stallybrass and White identify, usefully, "a striking ambivalence to the representations of the lower strata (of the body, of literature, of society, of place) in which they are both reviled and desired," an ambivalence that includes both "repugnance" and "fascination," Bellamy illuminates the gendered nature of the hierarchies of high and low culture and emphasizes the inextricability of repugnance and fascination in the particular case of the simultaneously shameful and desired female body.[15]

In a recent reading of Bellamy's work, Christopher Breu positions it as part of "a 'minor' practice of postmodern writing that engages with the obscene, abjected and disavowed materials of late-capitalist existence," a "counter-tradition" that "is often called the 'literature of transgression' and is associated with writers such as William Burroughs, Thomas Pynchon, J. G. Ballard, Samuel Delany, and Kathy Acker."[16] He contrasts this "late-capitalist literature of materiality" with more "immaterial" metafictional practices.[17] Breu reads Bellamy's work as "[articulating] an explicitly feminist and queer politics of materiality and embodiment, one that affirms rather than recoils from those aspects of our existence marked as

abject, disruptive, and all-too material" and as "[juxtaposing]
the theoretical and the intimate, the abstract and (representations
of) the brutely material in order to produce a discomfort that is
simultaneously stylistic and affective."[18] The "brutely material"
carries with it the shameful taint of the debased and coarse—again,
what is refused are the distancing gestures and self-consciousness
of intellectualism or of any position of moral superiority—and the
"discomfort" produced exemplifies the transmissibility of shame, its
highly contagious nature.[19] In confirmation of this point, Bellamy has
claimed that she "often [writes] about material I feel resistance to,
material that makes me uncomfortable, because that creates a charge
for me, a sort of erotics of disclosure."[20] If this "erotics of disclosure"
implies a (shameful?) pleasure on the part of both writer and reader,
the persistence of discomfort and the admission of vulnerability
make this a much more ambivalent experience than the *affirmation*
of the abject that Breu finds in Bellamy's work. That action of
affirmation is also troubled, I suggest, by Bellamy's undermining and/
or disorientation of the authority of the speaking "I" in much of her
work—most notably in those works employing cut-up.

Cunt-Ups (2001)

In *La seconde main ou le travail de la citation* (The Second Hand or the
Work of Citation) (1979), Antoine Compagnon praises the brilliance
and potential of the practice of citation:

> Blessed citation! Among all the words in our vocabulary,
> it has the privilege of simultaneously representing two
> operations, one of removal, the other of graft, as well as
> the object of these operations—the object removed and the
> object grafted on, as if the word remained the same in these

two different states. Is there known elsewhere, in whatever other field of human activity, a similar reconciliation, in one and the same word, of the incompatible fundamentals which are disjunction and conjunction, mutilation and wholeness, the less and the more, export and import, decoupage and collage? The dialectic of citation is all-powerful: one of the vigorous mechanisms of displacement, it is even stronger than surgery.[21]

In *Cunt-Ups* (2001), that "dialectic" is complicated, its possible synthesis disrupted, by Bellamy's practice of splicing together apparently incompatible materials (semantically, aesthetically, generically, and politically incompatible) in a manner that emphasizes disjunction, even while exploring the seamless conjunction and transmutation of bodies and body parts; there is no "reconciliation" here but rather a tireless process of juxtaposition and discordance that emphasizes the jarring joy and shame of desire. As Jennifer Cooke explains the method of *Cunt-Ups*:

> The source texts . . . were a mixture of Bellamy's own writing and some work by unnamed others; these were then subjected to the cutting technique that Burroughs specified by slicing each page into four. Each cunt-up includes a mixture of these different squares which were then taped together, typed up, and "reworked."[22]

Despite her initial misgivings about cut-up—"It seemed to me that only someone who had no access to an intuitive sense of reality would need to cut the text and tape it back together to get to this non-linear place. It seemed, in my reductive view of things, a very male thing to do a cut-up"—Bellamy decided to "[use] pornographic

material for my cut-ups and [rename] the form 'cunt-ups,'" claiming
that "It's a joke, but it's also a feminist reclaiming of the cut-up."[23]
In *Cunt-Ups* Bellamy uses the cut-up method "to enact the
interconnectedness between body and thing, to create a frenzy
of desire that subverts any stable abstraction of the lover's body
as object,"[24] which is here revealed in all its "brute"— sometimes
titillating, sometimes disgusting —materiality. She takes the material
from her "lovers' pornographic rantings," from "the language of critical
theory or abstraction," and from the confessions of serial killers
such as Jeffrey Dahmer.[25] In this way, irreconcilable discourses and
registers are compelled to co-exist—indeed, to conjoin; boundaries
between the proper and the improper, between high and low, are
irremediably transgressed.

The pornographic element is to the fore, with the text's ceaseless
repetition of "cunt," "cock," "asshole," etc.—a peppering of obscenity
that is, by turns, comical, discomfiting, embarrassing and titillating.
Whether or not *Cunt-Ups* is, as Bellamy claims, an attempt to "[take]
back" the "male form" of pornographic language and "[subvert] it to
my own ends,"[26] its jarring obscenities force us to consider language
as a tool of both violence and arousal (sometimes simultaneously),
while raising questions about what, precisely, constitutes the obscene,
the unspeakable, or the shameful. This sexualized language makes
the text also, in Cooke's reading, a "failure"—though this is not
presented as a criticism. As Cooke explains:

> Our words for sex are crude and *Cunt-Ups*, as its title
> suggests, knows this well. As a sensory experience, sex is
> hard to capture in language . . . . In this respect, *Cunt-Ups*
> necessarily fails and that is part of the point. As the text
> says itself, "No language will ever fit, no language will give

light to the mysteries of my overwhelming need to tell you
that I want" [from "Cunt-Up #17"]. Sex, then, would be a
limit case for representation, a threshold where language
falters or is impoverished. At the same time, language can
reach out and make you react, turning you on.[27]

Elspeth Probyn has claimed that "a form of shame always attends
the writer. Primarily it is the shame of not being equal to the
interest [in Tomkins's sense] of one's subject."[28] In the writing
of sex, that shame "of not being equal to" is magnified, and the
writing carries with it various additional varieties of possible
shame: at the "crude" (in all senses: unrefined, rudimentary,
imprecise, coarse) nature of sexual language; at the "failure" truly
to capture the "sensory experience" of sex; at the impossibility,
for Bellamy, of expressing her "overwhelming need"; at the social
and/or moral impropriety of the utterance of carnal desire itself
(particularly by a woman writer); at the (un)artistic taint of the
pornographic within the literary (the "low" sullying the "high");
at the unpredictability of arousal, when language "[reaches]
out and [makes] you react." Desire emerges here as voracious,
all-consuming: the one who desires is consumed by this desire,
unable to think of anything else (desire is thus simultaneously
agency and passivity, liberation and constraint); but the desire
itself is also a desire to consume, to ingest/incorporate the body
of the other. The second half of "Cunt-Up #4" repeats the phrase
"I want" eleven times: "I want to milk your come. . . . I want to
split you in half . . . , I want to take your skin off," etc.;[29] while
"Cunt-Up #13" declares, "It's like my cunt starts in the middle of
my chest. It's like there's a heart that's fibrillating, sucking in my
breath."[30] The final Cunt-Up ends, appropriately, with the sub-
clause: "my wanting."[31]

The presentation of violence and obscenity in *Cunt-Ups* is complicated further by the fact that it is near-impossible to discern, at each point, who is doing what to whom; there are no stable subjects (or even subject-positions) here, and thus no easy attributions of victimhood or tyranny; any sense of shame is, consequently, scattered, unattributed (though not thereby absent). Instead, organs are interchangeable, free-floating, and bodies refuse to cohere into "male" or "female"; shifting pronouns disrupt the ownership of bodies and actions. There is at work, instead, a diffuse agency, such that it is hard to tell who is active and who passive: "I contact either myself or you, I recall being involved at this time when I moved our hand across my body."[32] Cut-up and collage—or what Bellamy refers to elsewhere as "procedural practices and appropriation"—thus become "tools to break open and challenge the ego-driven narrative."[33] The dispersal of ego facilitates, in turn, a dispersal of both desire and shame—again, their *dispersal* rather than their *disappearance*. In the graphic prose-poems of *Cunt-Ups*, desire becomes flexible and free-floating, and bodies are endlessly changeable and permeable, penetrated and penetrating:

> My thoughts flutter down your purple neck and that gives
> me a hard-on. Your hips hugged against my belly, be inert,
> be happy, I just want to feel you with both feet overhead, all
> my fight waits to fuck your swollen pink and white spaces, to
> jostle you around gently until you turn blue. I kiss your finger
> and touch the head of your cock, you're wild now, invisible.[34]

The aggression here—"fight," "fuck"—is intermingled with tenderness; even spaces are materialized ("your swollen pink and white spaces"), lack becoming flesh. Yet the "purple neck" and "swollen pink" evoke bruising as well as arousal, and the text repeatedly returns to imagery of dismemberment: lovers becoming killers and their victims and vice versa; the body taken apart by desire, endlessly penetrated and invaded by the other.

> All these parts coalescing into a heart, we had sex and
> used sleeping pills, rose, and your cock in the center
> fucking, strangled me and then dismembered my body
> for the first time.[35]

In "Cunt-Up #4," she writes, simply: "I'm getting quicker at cutting up the body I was born with," suggesting the critical compartmentalization of the female body, its brutal objectification, as well as more literal violences enacted upon it.[36] All organs become sexual here, and every part of the body is open to the lover's touch—but also to violation: "your cock pokes up, divining my guts, my heart, my lungs, the undersides, I have no right to my organs, their incorrect shapes and desire."[37] This is a radical, uninhibited, unconstrained intimacy, a merging of bodies, but one that threatens a dissolution of self, and always carries the risk of injury: "I'm going to kiss you and when you fall asleep I'll stab you like a knife."[38] The surface "vulgarity," then, conceals a radical vulnerability, a sense of self-as-wound.

The dismemberment at the level of theme is also, of course, enacted by the text itself as a product of dis- and re-memberment, and Bellamy's practice of cut-up produces a kind of obscenity by juxtaposition.[39] As David Banash argues, "cut-ups do conceptual, aesthetic, and quite literal violence to ideas of writing";[40] here that "violence to ideas of writing" is used to explore—without reflective, redemptive, explanatory, or moralizing commentary— the violence that bodies do to each other, the pleasures and pains of embodiment, the violence of language, and the discomforts of

obscenity; the text is "perverted"—in various senses. As Bellamy
has commented on her practice of collage, "I often change such
stolen passages to the first person, I absorb and pervert them, make
them *me*";[41] this absorption, however, does not amount to anything
as settled and authoritative as ownership. Edward Robinson, in his
history of cut-up, asserts that:

> [i]ntegral to the nature of breaking down the control system
> were the random and collaborative aspects of the approach
> to the [cut-up] experiments. The random factor meant that
> not only was the control language held over the writer being
> broken down, but also the control the writer has over the
> words is diminished.[42]

This surrendering of "control," this refusal of the claim to full
authorship (and full authority), might suggest that cut-up—and
other forms of appropriation—has limited appeal for women authors
still trying to find a voice, to claim a right to speak or write, and to
establish their authority, and yet, for Bellamy (and for crucial female
forebears such as Kathy Acker),[43] it represents a deliberate violation
of the sanctity of the male-authored text and a protest against a
feeling of imprisonment within a patriarchal symbolic order. And
yet, again, despite the "aggressive" sexual explicitness of *Cunt-Ups*,
the blending and contortion of bodies and sentences models also a
kind of vulnerability—physical, emotional, sensual, artistic—to the
other; bodies and texts are intertwined, inextricable, interpenetrating
in a continual fluctuation of the sovereign and the subjected, the
shameless and the shameful.

Such dangerous fluidity is evident also in the way that the text runs
over with bodily fluids that might be the product of sex or violence, or

both, and that demonstrate a kind of exultation in abjection. These are leaky bodies that overspill their boundaries—as female bodies have stereotypically been held to do;[44] here, that unboundedness of bodies is gleefully ungendered. Cooke finds in *Cunt-Ups* "tenderness," "hard sex," "desire," and "love," as well as a lot about writing, but she also notes that:

> There's a lot in *Cunt-Ups* which is disgusting . . . . Disgust is contextual and sex is particularly good as a litmus test of this: what I might find disgusting with someone else, with my lover I find erotically charged, beautiful and exciting. Disgust, like lust, is a bodily affect, one that *Cunt-Ups* deliberately courts.[45]

What are the effects, for the reader, of the text's courting of the disgusting? Perhaps the point is that, in the absence of clear subject-positions, it is impossible to locate affects such as shame or disgust, or rather, any shame is taken on, worked through, by the reader. We feel addressed by, implicated in, the text—"Typing these words I was dragging your cunt behind me, you know it, you've wet everything we've touched, ripe like fallen fruit, like the earth," Bellamy writes, in "Cunt-Up #19"[46]—and for one critic of the later *Cunt Norton* (2013), "we feel guilty, like children caught touching each others' privates. To me, it's like Bellamy is my mother and my mother is watching me masturbate. She transforms me into one of her victims and accomplices."[47]

Bellamy's text raises questions, then, about what we might find personally disgusting or socially shameful, presenting embodiment and desire as experiences that oscillate unexpectedly (as her text does) between pleasure and shame; the depictions of bodies in

Cunt-Ups refuse aestheticization, abstraction or transcendence, preferring instead the carnal and animal. This is politically risky, given the cultural associations of female flesh with meat and the apparent shamefulness of such rapacious sexual appetites; indeed, Bellamy has elsewhere written about being a "bad experimental feminist," due to her commitment to "[addressing] raw emotion" in her work, in a way that is "embarrassingly nonfragmented and direct," and because "I was always eager to fuck."[48] If *Cunt-Ups* appears to privilege sex over emotion, Bellamy is nevertheless insistent that the cut-up technique is *not* a means of presenting "heightened emotion" that is "displayed but not owned," boasting instead that "in my writing I favor a direct assault of over-the-top emotion, hysteria even"; the use of "assault" hints at how excessive emotion becomes a weapon directed triumphantly outward, while "hysteria" unashamedly claims a conventionally feminized condition of disruptive, bodily feeling.[49] *Cunt-Ups*, accordingly, includes some moments of unexpected, uncanny lyricism and feeling:

> You don't know how infinite the course of my humiliations
> for you, singing actually—torch songs of nullity of being/
> being outside my kind of love, the kind of love the top of the
> wall carved a hole in. The rock. They opened the door, and
> tied me down, a runnel of water/a returned letter.[50]

Here, intimations of suffering and torture meet romantic cliché ("torch songs") and a shifting self/body transformed by desire. Yet despite describing *Cunt-Ups* as "a very romantic book" in which she is "collapsing romance and porn,"[51] Bellamy makes it clear that love involves a confession of unappeasable need and a reduction of self to "nullity" or object status that is ineluctably humiliating:

You can't see me because I'm still a thing. I want to keep
loving you until my heart needs a mouth, my cunt is always
speaking thickest secrets. I want to kiss you too, I want love
and longing, and your praises.[52]

the buddhist (2011)

In Bellamy's 2011 publication, *the buddhist*, it is "love and longing,"
rather than sexual desire, that are foregrounded, but the text
nevertheless deploys the twin approaches of vulnerability and
vulgarity as part of its exploration of the more shameful aspects of
embodiment and literary expression. *the buddhist* gathers together a
short, autobiographical story of the same title and a series of blog posts
from Bellamy's *Belladodie* blog. Together, these pieces chart the demise
and aftermath of Bellamy's relationship with a man identified only as
"the buddhist." The book combines elements of confessional memoir
with much self-reflexive musing on the writing of that story, alongside
commentary on Bellamy's day-to-day life and involvement in the
experimental poetry scene. In the course of the entries, she refers to the
blog as "my project of dailiness, endurance, embarrassment," and the
narrative, correspondingly, holds in tension revelation and boredom,
spontaneity and mundanity.[53] "As I continued the blog," she tells an
interviewer, "I came to view it as performance art."[54]

In *the buddhist*, Bellamy allows "emotional excesses to bleed around
my words" (the bodily metaphor again apparent), but she also explains
that, "I've tried to use my babbling about loss and betrayal as an
opportunity to refine and promote a political/aesthetic position."[55]
So "babbling" is validated as a kind of theorizing, and the personal
and subjective are put in the service of the political and collective,
exemplifying Bellamy's claim that "an in-your-face owning of one's

vulnerability and fucked-upness to the point of embarrassing and offending tight-asses is a powerful feminist strategy."[56] On this subject of vulnerability, Judith Butler, in a recent interview, asserts that "gender assignment finds us, from the start, vulnerable to its effects," and she figures vulnerability not as a form of "pure passivity" or as an absence of will, but rather as "the condition of responsiveness" that might lead to quite productive or positive challenges to "the terms by which we are addressed."[57] In Butler's reckoning, we are "vulnerable" in the sense that we are *subject to* the "enormous discursive practice" of gender, and vulnerable because we require these "forms of enabling address"—what she elsewhere refers to as *recognition.* In the case of the kind of disappointed/unreciprocated love narrated by *the buddhist,* that need for recognition—and therefore that vulnerability—is particularly pronounced, that "condition of responsiveness" particularly heightened. Recall Butler's claim, in *Undoing Gender* (2004), that we "are undone by each other. And if we're not, we're missing something. If this seems so clearly the case with grief, it is only because it was already the case with desire. One does not always stay intact."[58] Bellamy's refusal to "stay intact" is evident in her "owning" of her "vulnerability and fucked-upness" but also in the deliberately fragmentary nature of her text. For Butler, a rejection or denial of vulnerability is linked to "fantasies of sovereignty" (at the state level but also at a personal level); in texts such as *Excitable Speech* (1997) and *Precarious Life* (2003), she "endorses an engagement that is anchored in and arises from acknowledgment (not disavowal) of human interdependence and incompletion," an acknowledgment of our vulnerability, our susceptibility to injury at the hands of the other.[59]

In its candid acknowledgment of vulnerability in a manner that attempts to deploy that vulnerability as a feminist strategy of shaming, *the buddhist* can be read alongside texts that are formally

very different, such as Chris Kraus's *I Love Dick* (1997), Marie Calloway's
what purpose did i serve in your life (2013), or the artist Sophie Calle's
project/installation *Take Care of Yourself* (2009) at Paula Cooper
Gallery.[60] These works explore and document (rather than "confess")
experiences of romantic injury and vulnerability, shame and self-
abasement. Anna Watkins Fisher has discussed Kraus and Calle
as practicing a kind of parasitism, and she asks "how parasitism
might articulate itself as an experimental art practice as well as a
performance model for contemporary feminist politics"; both Kraus
and Calle, she argues, "[perform] the figure of the parasite as a figure
of overidentification," insisting on "loving men who reject them."[61]
Bellamy does something similar in *the buddhist*, finding a renewal of self
and renaissance of creativity in the apparent shame of her rejection:

> Over and over I'm finding that after the lover leaves, from a
> reader's perspective, that's when things get really exciting,
> for that's when a woman can finally settle into herself. It's as
> if the absent lover creates an opening to surprising depths of
> humanness.[62]

Furthermore, like Kraus—who cites the crucial influence of the
feminist body artist Hannah Wilke upon *I Love Dick*—Bellamy
declares that "what I'm doing here resonates with the history
of feminist performance art,"[63] referencing the work of Carolee
Schneemann, whose "interior scroll" (the paper slowly pulled from
her vagina during the 1975 performance of the same name) riffs:

> I met a happy man, / a structuralist filmmaker . . . he said
> we are fond of you / you are charming / but don't ask us / to
> look at your films / . . . we cannot look at / *the personal clutter*
> / *the persistence of feelings* / *the hand-touch sensibility.*[64]

In *the buddhist*, Bellamy marshals her "personal clutter" and gives her "feelings" full sway, but the "personal" is transformed via her "noisy corporeality" and the deliberate "vulgarity" of her writing.[65] She thereby inserts her work into a tradition of feminist avant-gardism that extends through poetry, prose, and conceptual art, taking in Kathy Acker's "aggro assertion of female subjectivity—aggro deconstruction of female subjectivity—aggro fuck you to received notions of female subjectivity,"[66] and Sylvia Plath's "exultation in lowness":

> [Plath's] "high" poetry may be formally brilliant, but
> its content embarrasses. Her domestic squabbles, her
> depression, her female rages. From her I learned to grope
> around in the dark muck of femaleness, to embrace the
> terrors and embarrassments that emerged.[67]

We might note here how the "dark muck of femaleness" is bound up with "embarrassment": the shame of the (merely) personal ("domestic squabbles"), the shame of excessive emotion ("depression," "female rages"), and, it is implied, the more primal shame of the female body itself ("the dark muck").

In connecting these experiences to the structural conditions of gendered vulnerability by situating their work in relation to a tradition of feminine and feminist self-exposure, artists such as Kraus, Calle, and Bellamy touch on a "primary vulnerability" with very particular social and cultural consequences for women. Such a primary vulnerability also works against a kind of sovereignty at the level of the self and of the text—hence the foregrounding of a shame that both produces and undoes the self; hence the texts' formal and other incoherencies (the text itself is "undone"); hence the disruption of any kind of stable narratorial "I"—while exploring qualities of "interdependence and incompletion." That vulnerability is, however, in Bellamy's work, always in tension with what she describes as the "feral." Asked about the graphic sexual content of her work, Bellamy avers that "all I ever wanted was to be feral, feral for me equals writing—my problem has always been how to enact the feral in a bourgeois world I wasn't raised to navigate."[68] To be "feral" means for Bellamy the embracing of pornographic imagery, a blurring of genres, a *shameless* mixing of high (poetic) and low (pornographic) content, but it also indicates a variety of sexual insatiability or voraciousness:

> My cunt flesh belches and fissures, torques itself inside out— this is the carnage of abandoned love—sex is dangerous, the buddhist told me over and over again—my cunt drools and spews, its juices glistening like a perfect orange on a rainy afternoon, my cunt shrieks never enough never enough never enough.[69]

Her unbounded body—emitting its "belches" and "juices" and "shrieks"—becomes, here, the locus of a vengeful, violent and limitless desire, obstinately insistent and inappropriate in its needs, its protests.[70] (This "carnage" has its detrimental effects, however: the passage hints at the bacterial infection with which Bellamy has just been diagnosed, so her "cunt flesh" expresses here both desire and disease.)

The opening "story" of *the buddhist*, by contrast, begins with a much tamer description of Bellamy having rather painful contorted sex with the eponymous subject of her narrative. There is little sense of shame in the scene or its narration, and Bellamy combines an awareness of the potential absurdity of the situation with a sense of its transformative beauty and power: "Upside-down, legs dangling

above me, I'm like an orchid hanging from the branch of a banyan
tree in a botanical garden in Florida, an extraterrestrial white flower
with a flushed pink core glowing in the generic hotel room light."[71]
In this description, the natural and fecund (orchids, banyan trees,
botanical gardens) wilt somewhat in the glare of the ersatz and
kitsch (the "generic hotel room light"), yet the "flushed pink core"
of Bellamy's desire dominates. Nevertheless, a friend asks her, "Are
you really going to get naked with him—at your age?" recommending
something that she calls a "post-menopausal sex burqa," and Bellamy
herself subsequently brands this opening story "a piece so obscene
it makes my soul blush," despite the fact that it is less candid than
other episodes in *the buddhist* and considerably less sexually explicit
than much of her other writing.[72] The question of what is appropriate
for a woman of her "age" resurfaces at several points in the narrative,
with Bellamy noting that "Middle aged women are such easy prey,
like they're supposed to walk around with eyes averted, hanging their
heads in shame at their wreckage."[73] This Bellamy defiantly refuses to
do, instead expressing the contradictory desire:

> To embrace the fucked-up, to move towards a maturity
> and strength that can include and express weakness and
> embarrassing content of all sorts without shame, to allow
> myself the full resonance of being a female subject . . .
> living in a fucked up nation, in a fucked up world, in the
> 21st century.[74]

To be "fucked up"—and to confess this—is, here, no barrier
to "maturity and strength," while Bellamy implies that the
foregrounding of "weakness" and "embarrassing content . . . without
shame" expresses the experience of "being a female subject . . .
in the 21st century." Vulnerability, weakness, and embarrassment

are thus reworked as positions of strength and possibility, while Bellamy's intensely personal, acutely emotional experiences speak to the structural inequalities facing women in respect to their bodies and desires. When Bellamy asserts, "To deny behaviors and experiences gendered as weak or 'feminine' is not feminist or queer, it's heteronormative to the hilt. Like Kathy Acker, I long to quiver and terrify in the same gasp," her juxtaposition of quiver/terrify similarly posits a model of female agency that combines vulnerability and confrontation or, more radically, stages vulnerability *as* confrontation.[75]

Despite elsewhere describing her work as "a user-friendly experimentalism, with lots of narrative candy and humor, a sort of avant-garde lite,"[76] Bellamy nevertheless declares, "It was a long hard road for me to feel okay about the sort of straightforwardness I perform in *the buddhist*."[77] It is certainly narratively much more accessible than *Cunt-Ups* and *The Letters of Mina Harker* (1998); what is carried over from these earlier works, however, is Bellamy's beliefs that "conceptual practices don't remove the self—they're Rorschach blobs into the self" and that "the conceptual—especially in the work of women—[cannot] be separated from the body."[78] The leaky, recalcitrant, uncontrollable, borderless, desiring/demanding feminine body (in Bellamy's presentation of it) is here mirrored by the mutating, disorienting syntax of the text, by its mix of the erudite and the vernacular, by its abrupt, discomfiting shifts between desire and disgust. Of course, the centrality of the body to women's conceptual art and writing has proven to be a contentious source of debate, as I have discussed elsewhere,[79] with Jennifer Ashton bemoaning the fact that "the new women's poetry understands 'innovation' as a direct extension and production of women's bodies," on the one hand, and Jennifer Scappettone retorting that for "women vanguardists," "the return to the body—which involves no unmediated return to a body proper—is a provocative feature of poetry riotously opposing a culture that continues to cast women as certain kinds—peculiarities—of subjects."[80] In Bellamy's case, the graphic, uncompromising communication of desiring, imperfect, voluptuous female carnality constitutes precisely both a stylistic and a political provocation; it forms part of her project of staging both vulnerability and vulgarity as offense and thus reworks feminine debasement as an experimental feminist strategy. As she explains in an essay entitled "Body Language":

> I'm particularly intrigued by writing that addresses the
> body—illness, ingestion, desire, display, sexual passion,
> subtle eroticism. The writers I most admire celebrate
> vulgarity and emotion . . . . Writing can and should offer an
> emotional engagement with materiality. That engagement
> can be highly mediated or direct, but that engagement
> begins a politics, a morality of writing.[81]

In *the buddhist*, what is embarrassing—even shameful—is not the candid, occasionally vulgar, language, or the engagement with the "brutely material" (to hark back to Breu's description), but rather the owning of desire and the speaking of emotion (the investing/ imbuing of materiality *with* emotion), betraying an "interest" (in the Tomkins sense of the term) that refuses to be cowed. In one episode, Bellamy takes an Ambien and "brainstorms" in her journal, offering us disconnected fragments of thoughts and feelings:

> As an antidote to my urge to privilege bookish mode over
> bloggish mode, here are my journal rants, typed up, as
> unedited as possible. . . . Notion of embarrassment—
> pushing towards discomfort. . . . I love the idea of giving

the impression of the unmediated in writing—to type in all caps WHY WON'T YOU FUCKING LOVE ME.[82]

The "notion of embarrassment—pushing towards discomfort" is notably unattributed—whose embarrassment, whose discomfort, is at stake here? If Bellamy is content to pour out her own minor humiliations in an "unmediated" way (or rather: in a way that gives "the *impression* of the unmediated"), she also uses this as part of her attempt to "[seduce] the reader into profound discomfort."[83] The narrative's metamorphosis from blog to book also allows Bellamy to reflect upon what constitutes "real writing" ("bookish mode," as distinct from "bloggish mode") and to see the gender bias in this: while male poets may be able to present their "letters and journals" as part of their "writing practice," she wonders:

> Would these guys consider a woman blogging about her heartbreak as part of a serious writing practice? I doubt it. Is my refusing to consider this blog Real Writing an internalized misogyny? My posts are too slight, too femmy, too sloppy (I'm a compulsive reviser), too easy.[84]

Yet she subsequently concludes that "the difference [between blog and book] isn't about value—one form isn't more valuable than the other—the difference is about labor and intensity,"[85] and the very form of the blog—its open-endedness, its participation in collectivity as her readers respond and empathize, its unfiltered, immediate quality, its multiple false endings (repeatedly she says, "its time to wind up the buddhist vein," before going on to write yet more about him)[86]—these qualities allow Bellamy the kind of emotional working-through that the end of the relationship with the buddhist requires. Eventually she must let go, declaring, "I can no longer hang on to the buddhist—the book, the person, or the blog. May I be wiped clean of all griping, abandonment, desire, melancholy, and rage."[87]

For Bellamy, the writing of *the buddhist* allows her to fashion her personal narrative as simultaneously emotional catharsis and social commentary:

> Writing about the buddhist here has been public display, of course, but it's been a public display of trying to figure something out, I'm not sure what it is—something about desire, obviously, and the trajectory of mourning—but also about boundaries, about secret/public, about embodiment and meaning, and the frailty of the ego, about the embarrassment and shame of being left or rejected, about pushing myself into ever uncomfortable spaces in writing.[88]

Shame—the "shame of being left or rejected"—is not only the subject matter here; it is also stimulus for and consequence of the "public display" of the text; "public display" indicates, in particular, the functioning of shame as spectacle, as a particular way of *being seen*. Shame speaks both to this testing of "boundaries" and to this engagement with the contradictions, the combined pleasures and terrors, of "embodiment" and selfhood ("the frailty of the ego"); finally, shame also becomes a *mode* of writing here, a narratorial policy of "pushing [oneself] into ever uncomfortable spaces." Importantly, Bellamy herself is not untouched by this—by the shame of what and how she writes—finding herself sometimes "unexpectedly mortified" when giving a reading.[89] As she explains in "Low Culture":

> I'm working towards a writing that subverts sexual bragging . . . .
> A female body who has sex writing about sex—no way can I

stand in front of an audience reading this stuff and maintain
the abstraction the "author" A BODY some writers glory in
this but I feel miserable and invaded—as if the audience has
x-ray vision and can see down to the frayed elastic on my
panties. But, really, it is I who have invaded my own privacy.[90]

Writing, then, does not release Bellamy from shame; there is nothing
triumphalist, consolatory, or straightforwardly redemptive in her
take on the debasements of the feminine. Bellamy refuses to disavow
the uncomfortable visibility of the "female body who has sex writing
about sex"; she refuses to separate body and text or to take refuge in
"the abstraction the 'author.'" I began this essay with Probyn's claim
that "bringing the dynamics of shame and disgust into prominence"
could facilitate "a more visceral and powerful corporeal politics"
and a more productive awareness of "the body's capacities for
reaching out and spilling across domains that we would like to keep
separate, or hidden from view."[91] As I hope I have shown, Bellamy
keeps little to nothing "hidden from view," and the dynamics of
shame and disgust form the larger part of her subject matter and
mode of expression. In forcefully confronting her readers with her
own, particular, vulnerability—in allowing that vulnerability to
spill out of the text, shamefully, inappropriately, vulgarly even—she
emphasizes our own "primary vulnerability," our own, necessary,
"interdependence and incompletion," as Butler phrases it, thereby
figuring writing as affective community. And in choosing to "[invade
her] own privacy," she acknowledges the formative, ineliminable role
of shame in both the public and private constructions of femininity
and in the act of writing.[92]

Re: Friedship between PB + KK

6/12/85

We will be ~~friends~~ together, no matter
who or what or who comes between us because
They can't touch it.   Signed —

                                    X Kevin Killian

                                    X Dodie Bellamy

First We Take Manhattan!

DODIE BELLAMY
AND
KEVIN KILLIAN

WILL READ FROM THEIR
PROSE AT EAR INN, 326
SPRING STREET, NYC, ON
SATURDAY, MAY 4, AT 3:00 P.M.

relentless? oral? phantom? cinema? laugh? inpenetrable?
doll? x-ray? bitter?
paranoid? suck? night?
x-rated? Long Island?
whispers? Bowie?
thighs? Cronenberg?
swell? homo? sparklers?
finger? burrito? fictions?
kiss? panties? kink? refrigerator? cool! glamor?
lyricism? me? jugular? futon?

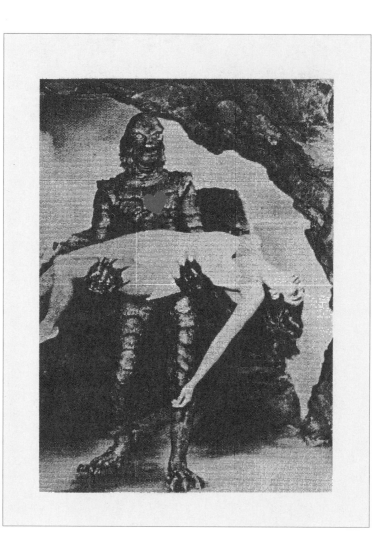

To Erwin, my true love —

... they want to put his delicate skeleton in a
glass case but he doesn't know he's exotic
flickering with the seaweed oxygen tank beneath
his horned spine hidden watching the beautiful
scientist's legs kick and arc so long and pearly
not even a callus on the heel his love for her is a
green jewel its red ghosts shifting in the third
dimension he has never seen anything so naked
doesn't know his scales would shred those thighs
those wavering arms the blood fanning out in
veils he reaches up half flipper half opposable
thumb opens at her ankle ...

Happy Valentine's Day!
Love, Dodie

CLUB
KEVIN & DODIE

Kevin Killian and Dodie Bellamy

are moving to San Francisco's

trendy, artistic SOMA District

As of September 14, 1991, their new address will be:
1020 Minna, San Francisco, CA 94103
New phone: 415/863-6798

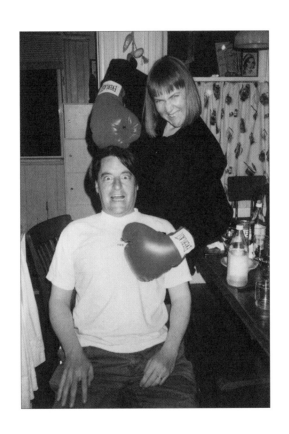

June 22, 1985

Mr. Kevin Killian:

How dare you tell Dodie you like her better than me, how dare you indulge in this
shocking promotion of sibling rivalry?
You're the evil step mother and Dodie's
your slovenly daughter and all I do is
push around the ashes, a girl with a glass
heart instead of a slipper. You shattered
it in that damned word processor, the
whirring daisy wheel pounding me black
and blue. To think we began this corres-
pondence with _pretty_ flowers. I GAVE YOU
MY DEWY AND QUIVERING AND YOU CALLED ME A
MAGPIE! Paper Stone Scissor--they're all
the same, something to hurl at the innocent
in the spirit of Shirley Jackson. These
paper cuts all over my face and fingers,
the way they itch and ache, the scabs thin
as capillaries, so delicate and dainty
you'd swear it was scrimshaw instead of a
human cheek.

Leaving aside your transparent attempt at
denial, how dare you judge my vision as
wrong _or_ right? I, Mina Harker, do, have
always and will always see through the
logical by means of the imaginal, leave
the intentional for the ambiguous. But
all you Kevins wouldn't understand, being
a quartet of phenomenological reductivists.
Quartet: meaning square, meaning a box
that locks you in so tight even Houdini
couldn't help you.

WHY DON'T YOU WANT TO LOVE ME?

Sincerely,

Mina

p.s. Please tell me the name of the
hidden god (*deus absconditus*) that you
follow.

                        --M

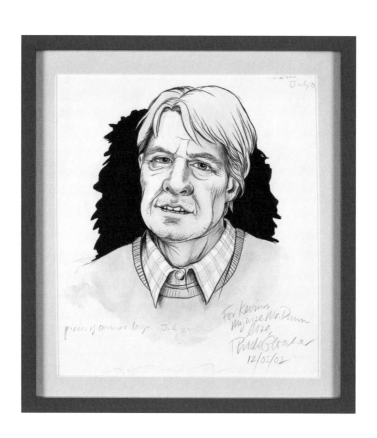

June 24, 1985

Kevin:

Here's your copy of our agreement; do you
remember it or were you hypnotized or are
you a victim of soap opera amnesia?

Are we going to seal it with a blood
ritual per discussed or is that too juvenile
for you in the light of the sun? I'm up
for it; I haven't done a ceremony with
anybody since Lynn when we went to a magic
circle by the ocean and threw things in
the water and burned a photograph of the
very spot in which we were standing.
Kevin, it would be like stepping into one
of your true crime books, but hopefully
with a better ending--I for one have no
intention of dying of a puncture wound,
etc.

Let me know--after two weekends of weddings
we deserve to do something not boring,
something that isn't about <u>families</u>,
it would even be better if it were
dangerous, but I wouldn't ask that
of you. But then, blood is always
dangerous--that's the whole point

of my book. You see I have all these
exacto knives--it would be much healthier
to use them on a finger instead of a wrist.

This is a real letter, so I'm not making
a xerox of it. And keep this in mind:
this isn't Mina who's talking, it's me,
Dodie.

Love,

Dodie

Kevin and Dodie

I know the butterfly is my soul grown weak from battle.
—John Wieners

WEEK 1, APRIL 28, 2019
Origins (Dodie)

DB: So, here are the parameters of this project, which I proposed to you. We will aim for a target of one thousand words a week for a year. If we go over that, fine, but one thousand is enough. Each week will have a topic, which we will take turns choosing. Whoever chooses the topic begins the dialogue. There are no limitations as far as topics go. They can include the present, the past, gossip, ideas, art, etc. This week I chose "Origins"—the history of our endeavors to write a book together.

KK: This is an amazing update of a project we began—and failed at—I don't know how long ago. Fifteen years? No, longer. I know! It was the week Wieners died. March 2002. We had proposed what seemed like a great idea to Lyn Hejinian and Travis Ortiz to write a volume for their newly launched press, Atelos. Everybody else was going to write poetry or theory, but you and I had been on the scene here in San Francisco for so long that we would just tell our memories of the things we had seen. We had the perfect title, *Eyewitness*.

DB: And then we tried a sample chapter, of our memories of John Wieners, who had just died. You're an avid collaborator, while I'm such a control freak; the process has never appealed to me that much. It seems to me that whenever you collaborate, the result sounds like a piece by Kevin Killian, and my ego is too big for that, though I've enjoyed writing copy with you for flyers and things like that. When I was the director of Small Press Traffic in the '90s, I remember us having a great time writing crazy copy for the flyers and reviews. And I got so good at your style that some of the most Kevin-esque passages were actually me doing a pastiche of you. So, we got through like a paragraph on Wieners, and the project became this object of discussion that never materialized—like George and Martha's phantom child in Edward Albee's *Who's Afraid of Virginia Woolf?*

KK: It was a disaster. It underlined totally how little we think alike and how differently we remembered basically the same events. It was so painful writing that one page that we never worked together again until we re-began work on our anthology of New Narrative writing. I remembered that we went on a cruise with John Wieners to get some "digestive aids" in North Beach on the rare occasion of his 1990 return to San Francisco, after decades away. I think you and I still have a package of those "digestive aids" he was hunting for, which turned out to be a package of Life Savers candy. You could have bought it anywhere, but he wanted to go to one store.

DB: So, already I disagree with a few things you've said. In my memory, Lyn asked us to write a joint book, and our memoir was what we came up with. I remember going around dramatically telling people that everybody else got their own Atelos book, but I had to share mine with you, like I was just half a writer. Meanwhile, Rae

Armantrout had her own book. Pamela Lu had her own book, Leslie Scalapino had her own book, and on and on.

The Wieners Life Savers were multicolored. He bought a tube for each of us, and one of us ate their tube and one of us—probably you with your archival fever—saved their tube and eventually sent it with our archives to Yale. In my memory, we were walking through Chinatown with Wieners and Raymond Foye, either before or after we went for drinks at Tosca— and Wieners walked into a random store and bought the "aids." These details are minor, but in a conventional collaboration, what do you do with them other than fight with one another over stupid stuff?

KK: What I remember is in the years in which I stored Wieners's Life Savers in your dentist cabinet, and I'd open the drawer, looking for a pair of scissors or whatever, is that Life Savers go rotten. The package itself looked kind of dusty/dirty, melted, and every time I noticed this deterioration, it reinforced in me the idea that you and I should never write together.

I also am thinking now that when he was hunting for digestive aids, it was the height of the AIDS epidemic.

DB: His conversation, both at his reading for the San Francisco State Poetry Center and in private conversation, was highly coded, so your AIDS connection may be spot on.

KK: You and I and Raymond were racing after Wieners, who was leading us in a heraldic quest to save our lives, like the White Knight in *Alice in Wonderland*.

DB: So you don't think our talking here about candy is juvenile?

KK: Add into this, also, the fact that in the legend of Hart Crane, he was a rich man's son whose father had become wealthy from controlling the rights to Life Savers, and in many ways, Wieners saw himself as the son of Crane.

In our case, candy is not only a metaphor but one piece of solid evidence that the entirety of our interchange with John Wieners happened, and that you and I still had no way of describing our separate encounters with Wieners's genius, how he, among all poets of his generation, affected each of us deeply but in very different ways. In a way, we had each come separately to San Francisco to meet him. And working with him and Raymond for a close period was one of the defining moments of our lives as artists.

DB: So maybe that's why we're still together. I'm totally behind you on what you say about Wieners's genius, and, yes, he's had an enormous impact on my writing. When I wrote that piece dedicated to him, "Not Clinical But Probable," which was published in *City Lights Review*, I heard that at his own reading at the Poetry Project, Wieners read from my piece. And then there's the whole issue that since there was all this sex with schizophrenic poets in the piece, the rumors were flying that I'd had an affair with Wieners, as if one homosexual poet—you—weren't enough for me.

KK: Thus are legends born. But to write a book of our memories seemed like it was asking for trouble, and so we closed the page for twenty years. But then, in 2017, the artist Ugo Rondinone asked that we write a catalogue essay for his show at the Berkeley Art Museum— his first show in the Bay Area—*the world just makes me laugh* (June 29–August 26, 2017). Ugo instructed us to tape a candid conversation as we walked through the objects in the show.

DB: We did visit the show together and had a wonderful afternoon, but being writers, we faked the conversation. There was no taping. We just sat down at the computer and began our back-and-forth. And it was so pleasurable and effortless, and exciting. Mostly because we didn't have to agree on anything. Ugo said it would be interesting to hear our conflicting points of view, rather than a unified front.

KK: Maybe it was easy because Ugo's show was all about clowns. Clowns are amusing, childish, grotesque. They're not a subject to be taken seriously. And yet his treatment of this theatrical subject invited our own associations, not only of clowns we'd seen as kids, but as a subject for fine art over several centuries.

DB: That tension between wanting to risk foolishness yet wanting to be taken seriously seems to me central to both of our writing practices. Happily, both the artist and curator (Larry Rinder) approved of our text and asked for very few changes. So a few weeks ago, when we were again asked to write a joint catalogue essay (and the fact that anybody would want us to write a joint catalogue essay confuses me) for the Mike Kelley show that was recently at 500 Capp Street—*Mike Kelley: Pushing and pulling, pulling and pushing* (November 3, 2018–February 16, 2019)—you proposed another dialogue. And it was equally pleasurable to work on.

KK: Actually, the Capp Street curators wanted either of us or both, but I was incapable at that time of writing anything about Mike Kelley without your help because of my medical problems, so I needed you as never before, and you gave everything. In both these cases, it was fun because Ugo and Mike are among the favorite artists of both of us, which is weird because we don't agree on many things.

DB: And then I got the idea for this book and bugged the shit out of you until you agreed. Why did you finally cave in?

KK: The horror of the one paragraph of *Eyewitness* that we wrote was pleasantly balanced out by the great reception we've had for our anthology, *Writers Who Love Too Much: New Narrative 1977–1997*. Remember, that was a project posing many more dangers to our marriage than *Eyewitness*.

DB: But on the critical parts of the book, we didn't totally collaborate. You'd write; I'd read and give suggestions, and you'd write more. I feel like I was more of a developmental editor for that book. My input was integral, but I let you lead on the writing. And here we're going to try to perform as equals. For one year.

KK: I feel like opening that dentist drawer one more time and looking at that candy. But it's gone.

WEEK 2, MAY 5, 2019
Communal Presence:
New Narrative Writing Today (Kevin)

KK: I remember the excitement and the dread of Communal Presence, the New Narrative conference at UC Berkeley in the fall of 2017, which followed the publication of our *Writers Who Love Too Much* and Rob Halpern and Robin Tremblay-McGaw's *From Our Hearts to Yours: New Narrative as Contemporary Practice*. Two branches of the University of California (Berkeley and Santa Cruz) were joining forces and actually doing this. Ten years before, I don't think anybody thought of New Narrative as anything other than a failed experiment or, at best, a forgotten avant-garde.

DB: I don't agree that New Narrative was forgotten. There's been a history of younger poets taking it up, such as Dana Ward, and pushing its concepts into new directions, sometimes more poetic than what early practitioners worked in, even though the movement was founded by poets who didn't know how to write narrative. I remember asking Bob about some stupid formalist issue about "craft" my fiction students had brought up that I found oppressive, and Bob had never heard of it, though it was commonly taught in fiction workshops. And he seemed blessed to me, not having the burden of such toxic exposure. Until recently most of our invites to universities have been generated by grad students (rather than faculty), and the *Communal Presence* conference continued that trend.

KK: The coolest part is that we got to stay on campus at the Women's Faculty Club, a classic Julia Morgan building, teetering between mansion and dump, tucked into a corner of the campus few people knew about.

DB: It was next to Optometry or something.

KK: There we stayed, as if in a dorm, with the world's oldest students—Eileen Myles, Dennis Cooper, Nayland Blake, Carla Harryman, and on and on. So many friends, some of whom we'd grown apart from somewhat. We were reunited at last, like one of those '80s movies like *The Big Chill*, eating breakfast together, and it was in the middle of a horrible firestorm in Napa, and many wore surgical masks.

DB: The organizers did not intend to house locals at the Women's Faculty Club. We were only there because I threw a "diva" when I found out our panel was scheduled for 9 a.m., saying I couldn't possibly get from San Francisco to Berkeley that early. So their compromise was to give us a room and change our panel to 11 a.m. And so we're in Berkeley in the middle of all this smoke, which was milder in San Francisco, and I was missing the pricey air filters I have in our apartment, and it seemed like karma paying me back for being such a bitch.

KK: To an astonishing degree, organizers Eric Sneathen and Daniel Benjamin followed our roadmap of who we wanted to share the stage with us. Not necessarily the most famous writers but those our anthology insists are vital: Gabrielle Daniels, Michael Amnasan, Roberto Bedoya. Confounding everybody, we persuaded Judy Grahn to come—not a New Narrative writer herself, but a forebear.

DB: Judy Grahn's reading of her epic 1974 poem, "A Woman is Talking to Death," in the Maude Fife Room at Wheeler Hall, was one of the most powerful readings I've ever seen. People were stunned, brought to tears, hanging on every word. When she finished, I left the room and sat by myself in the lounge because nothing could follow that.

KK: She seemed to lose strength around part seven of the nine parts, like she was going to faint, and kept herself going through sheer force of will, but eventually her partner, Kris Brandenburger, helped her to her seat and finished the reading for her. Presently Grahn rose, gave a weak wave, and faced an insane crowd that had been driven mad by ecstasy, the spectacle of her dying and coming back to life in front of our eyes, I guess kind of an allegory for New Narrative itself in this context.

DB: I feel low-grade panic at all conferences, but at this one there were so many people I had complex histories with that needed to be negotiated, plus a couple of years before that I'd had the experience of being shunned and bullied by a group of East Bay poets, so I tend to avoid East Bay poetry events. I pretty much tried to erase myself from the whole conference. The big reading event with all us oldsters took place at the Omni Commons, which had been a focal space for the bullies. I gave a short, uninspired reading because I just didn't want to be up there. Despite my discomfort—and that godawful smoke—I found the weekend to be tender, with many cherished bits of conversation, and then there was that one panel I attended where one of the young women presenting kept mouthing to me across the room, "I love you."

KK: Then there was the drama of the bedbugs in our fabulous Julia Morgan residence. I think only Nayland got them bad and had to change rooms. There was something biblical, though, about the smoke and the pests, something from Leviticus. It was really like the end of the world. I remember introducing Nayland to Renee Gladman, who, remarkably, had never met. It was two eras colliding, finding a common space, a communal presence, I guess.

I understand, Dodie, that you were uncomfortable about the complexities of all the social interactions and, indeed, about what was happening in the outside world in that moment, basically the rise of Trump. My reactions were a little different, just a tide of disbelief that this was really happening, that hundreds of people came. Not just scholars but artists and musicians, filmmakers. Corin Sworn was there, do you remember, Dodie, all the way from Glasgow?

DB: No, I don't remember Corin being there, but when we got to know her a bit in Glasgow, and she was so great, I felt I'd missed a chance in

Berkeley, and I wondered how many other chances I let slip through my fingers due to my social whatevers.

KK: I want to talk about the hierarchy of the conference, how one evening we drove the estimable Brian Blanchfield back to where he was staying, and it was this crummy little hotel, way down University Avenue, halfway to the freeway, and how this reflected something of a caste system I will never understand. I mean caste system of academia.

DB: I get what you're saying in principle. Being an adjunct, I live and breathe from a lower rung in such a system, but we were the subjects of the conference, so it makes sense we'd be treated differently. But it's odd to be both subject and participant in something at the same time. Like, who are you? And the conference seemed to invite a sort of egomania that I think most of us were trying our best to resist. Not all, but most.

KK: And then there was the spectacle of Bruce Boone wearing lavish, blue eye shadow during his reading at the Omni. It was like what the hell. It was like a declaration from Bruce, yes, you haven't heard much from me for decades, but I am back, and I am a classic legend.

DB: Many of us had felt ourselves part of New Narrative—but had grown out of it. Michael Amnasan, though he's kept on writing, had cut off almost all contacts with a literary community. He wouldn't even answer our emails when we asked him to be in our anthology. Somehow, I found out his wife was a New York–based food blogger, so I looked up her blog and left a plea for Michael to contact us in the comments section of one of her blog posts. That worked.

But, anyway, there was an off-kilter feeling of being on the outskirts of a moment for years and then suddenly finding oneself sucked back into the center. Though "finding" is not really an accurate verb, since we edited an entire anthology promoting the subject. Like all the fairy tales warn, be careful what you ask for.

KK: And everywhere the ghosts of people who did not live to see this conference.

DB: That's the one thing I asked for that Daniel and Eric did not provide—some sort of panel or reading or remembrance for people involved with New Narrative who had died. Sam D'Allesandro, Bob Flanagan, Lawrence Braithwaite, Steve Abbott, Marsha Campbell, John Norton. Of course, some of these people were discussed in panels. Our ghosts.

KK: Ghosts in the smoke.

WEEK 3, MAY 16, 2019
Mortality (Dodie)

DB: I was planning to suggest a more fun topic, but after the last few days—the death of the artist Lutz Bacher and our visit this morning to the weird oncologist—there would be this huge elephant in the room if we discussed any other topic besides mortality. Are you okay talking about that?

KK: Not to mention the way the week started off, with the death of Peggy Lipton, whom I loved so much?

DB: Was she on *Mod Squad*?

KK: Yes, she was the one from *Mod Squad*, in the '70s, I guess. Julie. And also, to top it off, as though Peggy Lipton's death wasn't enough, Doris Day died within twenty-four hours. Funny thing is Doris also played in a movie called *Julie*. She was a stewardess with an abusive husband she was trying to escape. Louis Jourdan. He terrorized her on an airplane. People think of Doris as some kind of sexy virgin, trying to preserve her virginity, but she was often tormented and abused by the men in her life.

The other point about Peggy Lipton and Doris Day, blond American girls next door, is that they were race pioneers. Peggy shocked the world when she married the musician Quincy Jones, and Doris— much, much older and considered something of a square in the music world—allowed herself to be photographed behind a piano singing with Sly Stone in the pages of *Rolling Stone*. They were both dangerous women, or women dangerous to patriarchy.

Then there was Lutz Bacher. And then a simple phone call from Andrew Durbin made it clear that the world of death had come awfully close.

DB: Today you made jokes about what bad taste it was for Andrew to ask you, with your cancer diagnosis, to write an obituary as your entrance into *Frieze*. Did writing and thinking about Lutz highlight your own mortality, or did the process of pushing around words shield you from that?

Reading your piece made me long for the '90s San Francisco art scene, in a sort of tragic way. For me, even the fondest of memories are laden with a sort of death. The finality of their past tense and my rewriting them in my memory. Your quoting of a passage I wrote about Lutz, detailing something I had no active memory of. Even now, it's all kind of blurry and might as well have been a memory of a movie. Who lived that life? It doesn't quite feel like me.

KK: Out of the *Frieze* obituary, I left the most melodramatic story, as any responsible journalist would. As I remember hearing it, Lutz's professor-husband, Donald Backer, retired from UC Berkeley's Astronomy department, lost his health benefits and collapsed in 2010 outside their home, and Lutz is said to have blamed the university system for his death. According to Darrell Alvarez, when he and Lutz both had shows at the Berkeley Art Museum in 2012, Lutz never went to see her show, so linked was the university for her with Don's death. She sold her house for under market value, moved to New York, fired her Bay Area gallerist, and, in a spectacularly operatic gesture, never returned. Vengeful, haunted, she lived out the rest of her life in a haze of renunciation. Paradise had been lost. Bitterness took over.

DB: I love your novelization of Lutz's life post-Don, which you're spinning out of very little information. But I suspect you're seeing into some core truth she most likely hid.

KK: Maybe I'm just projecting because that's how I feel right now.

DB: But you've been so happy lately, in your partially steroid-induced bliss. You're not actively expressing these darker emotions. I'm the one in our relationship who holds the dark emotions.

KK: Oh, Dodie, you know every year I would write an Oscars column for *Fanzine*, and every year I was bitter, bitter that Doris Day had never won the honorary Oscar. Nobody took Peggy Lipton seriously either, until she returned to TV in middle age in *Twin Peaks*. People stopped laughing at Lutz when she showed emotion—before that she was like a clown, like a Sturtevant without brains, like a pathetic scamp—think of Giulietta Masina or Agnès Varda, sad sacks poking fun of themselves.

DB: Your metaphor is confusing me, because GM and AV sound like they're all about emotion.

KK: They're about downplaying emotion before other people can poke fun of them. And one gesture—all Lutz had to do was raise an arm and point a finger, and she became like Angelina Jolie in *Maleficent*, a terrible, rage-consumed creature seized with power.

DB: And so how are you projecting into all of this?

KK: My cancer diagnosis wouldn't have happened to me if I'd had a better attitude about myself, a more powerful sense of myself. If I had named names, instead of shrugging, when bad things happened to you or to me.

But I wanted to return to your lack of memory about your exchanges with Lutz. You didn't even realize she was one of the characters in your novel. You saw stills from her screen tests of you looking as ravishing as any screen goddess, and you said, *that can't be me*. What is erasure all about? It's not just death, it's . . . forgetting. It's not just forgetting, it's the inability to take in pleasure and a sense of one's own worth.

DB: Are you saying I can't take in pleasure?

KK: It has no permanent resting place in your psyche. But what am I saying—I just ate a whole candy bar, a giant candy bar, shaped like the map of California, like in the Jack Spicer poem "Psychoanalysis: An Elegy" (*I want to write a poem as long as California and as slow as a summer*), so maybe I'm kind of nuts right now. After going to the Joan Brown show at Anglim Gilbert this afternoon, we came home and spent half an hour weeping, hopelessly, because we were going to miss each other so much if the worst happens. And I said it may not happen for a long time. Both of us have a sense of ending, and that's one of our strengths as writers and thinkers.

How long did it take me to imagine the end of *Spreadeagle*? Twenty-three years? How long did it take you to finish *The Letters of Mina Harker*? Fifteen years? Sam D'Allesandro had to die. And when you were writing "In the Shadow of Twitter Towers," you thought it was finished, but nobody had died. Then Omar (the guy whose body was found in a suitcase) died, and your piece went on and on, gaining in power, gaining in horror, until you had set fire to the whole system of the city.

DB: I'm thinking of how Dennis Cooper said AIDS ruined death. It doesn't sound like your cancer diagnosis is ruining death for you, but that it's a generative thing.

KK: You and I lived through AIDS, and during those fifteen years, there was literally nothing but hopelessness, nothing but death.

DB: I disagree; it was also a wonderful time for community and art. And love. My heart was so open in those days.

KK: I think that there's more hope these days, so that there's less community, less art, less operatic passion.

DB: How can you believe that in the Trump era there's more hope? I find myself saying repeatedly, Capitalism is winning, Capitalism will always win. And it doesn't give a damn about us.

KK: Dennis's point is that once we were in love with death in the Punk era. It seemed like the real thing, the point of living. Then came AIDS, and death was reduced to nothing. Just the end. It was stripped of meaning.

DB: The act of growing old, which seems like such an impossible thing to have happened to me, makes mortality tasteable, like it's on my tongue. At this stage in life, its inevitability is so clear, and there's this constant sense of impending. How has getting ill impacted that sense for you? Is it the same but more heightened? Or is it a new feeling altogether? And I imagine this will shift over time, once you're getting treatments, etc.

KK: I think it's all those things. Let's wait a few weeks and see what happens. And, oh, Dodie, I have so much to say still about Peggy Lipton and Doris Day.

WEEK 4, MAY 18, 2019
Drawing (Kevin)

KK: I started making poem drawings when we heard that CA Conrad was trying to raise money for Frank Sherlock's hospitalization in Philadelphia around 2005. Frank had come down with encephalitis after spending weeks and months helping the people of New Orleans cope with the devastation of Hurricane Katrina. Or at least that's what we heard.

DB: When we saw him, he was frail and walking around with a cane and looked quite noble. People were stunned, and he was heavily romanticized.

KK: His black beard, like a pirate's beard. The beard was alive and so was the cane, but the rest of him was dead. He was a bouncer at a bar called Dirty somebody's. I remember the two of us being there.

DB: Did we go there more than once—because that's the place where I got into the fight with David Buuck, and the two of us stood outside screaming at each other, as the Philadelphia poets stood round, observing. It was similar in a way at the Orono conference on the poetry of the '50s, when Barrett Watten and Marjorie Perloff stood in a communal lounge and shouted into each other's faces about capitalism, and we stood round silently cheering as if at a boxing match. Except with David and me, there were no pretenses of it not being personal. You weren't on the trip, and David was supposed to take care of me, and I didn't think he was doing a good enough job, and every time he'd disappointed me since the mid-'90s came flooding back. Of course, after that drama, having released the steam of our tensions, our friendship has been sweet ever since.

KK: Maybe that's how Barrett and Marjorie feel.

DB: I don't think so.

KK: It was Conrad, Frank's best friend, who came up with the idea of getting the poets to write out a poem of their own and then to auction them off on eBay. Which seemed marvelously innovative at the time. This was before Kickstarter. When I saw the names of the other poets, I shrank like a butterfly. Conrad has powerful friends. Susan

Howe. Dottie Lasky. Colorful people. Like Dottie could bejazzle a poem with fake precious jewels glued to the piece of paper. What could I do? How could I compete? And so I decided to use Sharpies to draw pictures on my poem. I wouldn't type; I would write the words out by hand. Calligraphy.

DB: I might call it anti-calligraphy. I notice that this is like the fourth time in the past few days you've referred to butterflies. Which reminds me of a photo I saw the other day of a woman looking at a display of Nabokov's butterfly collection, which I find kind of creepy. Precise and creepy.

Butterflies are traditionally metaphors for the soul. Is the soul something you've had at the back of your consciousness lately?

KK: I remember going to Santa Cruz with you and stopping at this one grove of trees that was famous for looking like it was moving, like a million shadows were on it. It was crawling with butterflies. Billions of monarch butterflies would stop there on their way to South America.

DB: I was disappointed in them because I'd imagined this vivid orange, but what it mostly looked like was fluttering bark. They reminded me of those lumpy rock creatures in *Flash Gordon* that would jump out of the rugged mountainside.

KK: I think I did pretty well with my first poem drawing. It was called, "That Certain Something," from Kylie Minogue's French period, *Body Language*, with her imitating Jane Birkin and Serge Gainsbourg. I used bright Sharpies, the color of the Riviera. Yellow, green, purple. I didn't yet know how to draw anything, but I could underline. Years later, I had a call from Barbara Gladstone, the eminent New York gallerist, who told me that one of her artists had seen this loser thing on eBay and admired something about it, and that he wanted to work with me. He wanted me to develop this style, the style of the fluttering bark. In the interim I had done a writing workshop for kids, and I wrote a poem called "A/Butterfly." The third line began with a *C*, and the fourth line began with a *D*. In Nabokov's story, "The Vane Sisters," butterflies are the spirits of the sisters who in real life were mediums. And now they become letters of words. They are spelling out the hidden meaning of the story.

When I got sick and couldn't write, I went through my drafts hoping to find one last thing I could write, and I had written out the beginning "A / Butterfly," and I drew a butterfly, pale blue like a tear. The rest of the page was blank.

Did you ever like butterflies, Dodie, when you were a little girl, maybe?

DB: All kids like butterflies, but I do remember one landing on my flesh and finding it unnerving. I feel bad for butterflies that come in contact with humans, the way they're captured and kids pull their wings off. I'm thinking of some song from our youth, "The Iron Butterfly of Love." Or am I getting that wrong?

KK: The Iron Butterfly was a band. You're thinking of "The Elusive Butterfly of Love."

DB: We listened to Iron Butterfly's "In-A-Gadda-Da-Vida" the first time we did acid, because we thought that would set us in the proper mood. I was fine with it, but my girlfriend practically started convulsing with panic.

KK: Because of the music?

DB: I don't know. She often had a hard time on the stuff, but that didn't keep her from doing it over and over. Do you ever have a compulsion to repeat something that scares you / tears you up?

KK: You know I do. Like whenever we have a fight, I want to make it up. It's scary to want somebody so much.

DB: You're trying to sweet-talk me because I didn't want to write about drawing. I'm the worst drawer in the world.

KK: You're the reason they invented Photoshop, so you too could become a famous artist.

DB: You mean, the reason they invented fabricators. When I first heard about fabricators, I felt ripped off in life, thinking, *I would have gone to art school if I'd known you didn't have to be able to make anything yourself.*

KK: That freed me, I'd say.

DB: I'm realizing more and more that the literary world has never been a good fit for me. I've always wanted to hang out with the artists.

KK: What magazines did we have growing up? It wasn't *Butterfly*, it was *Caterpillar.* How dreary! A caterpillar is a cement mixer or truck or something.

DB: Isn't it the thing from which butterflies grow? Like the prototype of a butterfly?

KK: In art you don't need talent, all you have to have is gesture. In writing you need talent; it's all about what they call craft.

DB: I would say gesture is the supreme talent. Everything else is craftsmanship. Craft taught in writing programs destroys talent. When we were at that purposely unnamed group reading last night, the one person who showed talent was the spoken-word guy, whose work was so rough and all over the place. There were hints of the real, for lack of a better term.

An example of gesture versus craft would be Lutz's *Playboys* series. She hired an illegal Russian immigrant to paint the Vargas drawings. She said Russians could do anything. They could make rubber cement out of old tennis shoes. There were supposed to be more paintings in the series, but the project came to a screeching halt when Lutz showed some of the paintings, and to her horror, the Russian went and saw how much they were going for. He got all haughty and asked for more money since he was the real artist. He couldn't understand that in this scenario he was merely a channel—a sort of trance-medium manifesting Lutz's vision. But I feel for him, the unjustness of class systems and labor.

Recently I found out that—after teaching two classes a semester at San Francisco State for nineteen years—all it would have taken for me to enter the pension plan was to have taught three classes for three semesters in a row. After that, it wouldn't matter how many classes I taught. Once you're admitted to the plan, you're in for good, and you can buy back the time you lost and get a full pension. In those nineteen years, the female poet who was chair most of the time never offered me three classes, and now I'm having to fight for them. No matter how successful I become in life, in my heart I will always be Lutz's angry Russian.

KK: When Ugo told me—for it was Ugo Rondinone who had Barbara Gladstone call me—that he wanted me to draw pictures into my poems, I responded by saying I couldn't draw anything. He said—you can draw a smiley face, you can draw Hello Kitty, you can draw the rays of the sun, you can draw daisies and roses, and you can draw a butterfly. That's all you need.

DB: And, thinking of his clown show at the Berkeley Art Museum, you could also draw a rainbow. It was shocking how stunning it was, the room plastered with children's drawings of rainbows, floor to ceiling. It should have been totally cheesy, but it was marvelous, like jaw gaping.

KK: For me the '60s were Muhammad Ali, the greatest of all time: "Float like a butterfly, sting like a bee. The hands can't hit what the eyes can't see."

WEEK 5, MAY 26, 2019
Childhood Sex (Dodie)

DB: Our having gotten together and lasted so long was so unlikely, it makes me want to search for points of contact. Each of us grew up in the suburb of a large city—New York for you, Chicago for me. Both of us read incessantly as children (though that's true for most of the writers we know; it seems a recent phenomenon, non-readers wanting to become writers; I'm thinking of the many students in writing programs I've taught in who don't read books). We're both firstborns. We both have birthdays on holidays. And we both had sex as children.

KK: I should say that I wanted to have sex as a child, but I didn't often get to do it.

DB: But what about the Carey person you write about? Weren't you like fourteen when you became involved with him? How old were you when you first had sex?

KK: I was thirteen or fourteen when I had sex for the first time. It took me longer than that to learn how to come, but I wanted to find sexual fulfillment with another person. That was the purpose of life. Or so we thought, our generation. I was fourteen when I met Carey. I'd hitchhiked for a year before I landed him. I wanted someone approximately as old as my father, and almost as good-looking, and I landed on him, who matched my ideal mate in many ways and yet was also the exact opposite of what I wanted in a guy. I wanted somebody who was more like myself, my own age, my generation, with my interests, like a twin. I don't remember the first person I had sex with, but it was in the woods that surrounded my house. Probably neighbor boys, or boys from other parts of Smithtown, or strangers. I followed notes that were left in the trees, like leaves, promising sexual satisfaction. Later I realized that since childhood my reading had programmed me to look for eternal love.

What year was it that you first had sex? Were you around the same age?

DB: It was 1962, and I was eleven, and unlike you, I wasn't looking for sex; in fact I didn't know what it was; I didn't know how babies were conceived. I got involved with a predatory girl my own age who was coming on to all the other girls at sleepovers. I'm the only one who did it; we pretended to be asleep. I guess even though I didn't know what sex was, I had a strong libido. The first time she stuck a finger in my vagina, I came instantly, having no concept of what an orgasm was, but I remember thinking how all these things I'd been seeing in the world suddenly made sense, from Doris Day movies to bikini advertisements, to marriage. Everybody was flirting and preening to have this sensation, which felt good enough to drive you crazy.

And, yes, I too was programmed to connect sex with eternal love. I stayed in that relationship for fifteen years, though I'd say by the end of high school I was dying to get out of it. But I stayed. To compensate, I began a long history of cheating; that way I could be both inside a situation I was addicted to yet outside of it at the same time. Now that I'm older, I feel a lot of resentment toward her. I was too young to have sex, and being in a lesbian relationship with no support, as a child, years before Stonewall, in Indiana, was hell. It added another layer of otherness to the otherness I felt profoundly, always having been somewhat of a misfit. On the other hand, if I didn't feel otherness, I'd probably still be in Hammond, Indiana. So in a sense all that pain and alienation got me out of there, propelling me toward a richer life.

KK: Remember when we went to your twentieth high-school reunion? You could tell who the gays and lesbians were because they looked so good. And the regular people all looked like their parents. One woman asked me if I was "part of the family," and I didn't know what she meant. She got out quick. When high school ended, she moved to Chicago and designed interiors for McDonald's. All your other classmates were entering a contest about who had the oldest child. And who had come the farthest. And we had come from San Francisco, and people asked us how many children we had, and we just laughed, helplessly.

DB: And people kept saying to me, "Doris, you look so much better than you did in high school." Which was such a weird compliment, I didn't know how to take it in. It was a blast to sit at the queer table at the reunion and make fun of the other geeks who used to shun us.

KK: For some reason, everybody—and I mean like twenty people—at that gay table had all gone to Chicago, and all seemed to be intimate with the crime writer Sara Paretsky.

DB: From things you've both written and said, Carey treated you badly and introduced some sex kinks, such an enemas, that make me cringe, imagining them done to a little boy. Do you have resentment toward him? You pose yourself as the predator, but do you also see him as predatory?

KK: I wasn't a little boy, exactly. I thought of myself as a young man with a desperate hunger for experience and wisdom. In the years that followed, I saw more clearly how the system, how the multiple systems, propel themselves forward by institutionalizing what you might call adult-child sex. I do blame the adults, sort of, and I'm glad that I went on to adult sexuality as soon as I did.

DB: What do you mean by "as soon as I did"?

KK: Before I knew it—let me illustrate—the number-one song in the world the week I had sex for the first time was by the Beatles, a two-sided hit from 1966, both sides very experimental and strange. "Paperback Writer" on one side. "Rain" on the other. By the time I graduated from high school, it was David Bowie, Marc Bolan, and Lou Reed all the time. "You've got your mother in a whirl / 'Cause she's not sure if you're a boy or a girl." "Rebel rebel, you've torn your dress / Rebel rebel, your face is a mess." Experimental also, like the

Beatles, but with the focus resolutely turned to deviant sexuality. And that's where I stayed until I met you.

DB: Are you saying I made you wholesome?

KK: Just the opposite. But what was that T. Rex song about a diamond star halo? "You're an untamed youth / that's the truth / With your cloak full of eagles / You're dirty sweet / And you're my girl." That's you, Dodie. I dedicated *Bedrooms Have Windows* to you, Dodie, in 1988: "Girl, I'm just a jeepster for your love." There were these machine-world images of sexual desire—cars, motors, bombs, weapons—that promised hurt as well as salvation.

DB: I never listened to David Bowie until "Major Tom," but I was crazy about T. Rex and Marc Bolan. I remember he claimed he was going to change shape on stage, from one form to another. Unfortunately, I can't remember what the new form was supposed to be. He was a self-proclaimed mystic. But it was crazy back then, like my next-door neighbor, Jeff, who did a lot of acid, believed his car could drive itself. I think that's because he often didn't remember the journey. One time we went to see Jethro Tull in Frankfort, Kentucky, and we missed the turnoff and everybody was so stoned it took two hours for anybody to notice. There was a big flood and the concert was canceled anyway, and it was magical, driving through the ravaged landscape, horses standing in water, houses in water up to the second floor. No inkling of danger in the car, just this sense of time slowing down.

KK: We both lived with a lot of secrets: perhaps all young people do. Because we were writers, we could give up our shame and our covert sexualities easier than others among our peers, our forebears, and those who have come after us. It's strange to think that we might have been the luckiest generation to have lived in the twentieth century. And all because of that one song, "Rain," by the Beatles.

DB: My girlfriend's and my favorite song to have sex to in college was Blind Faith's "Can't Find My Way Home." Beautiful, but kind of a sad song. We didn't know what we were doing.

I've never chosen to be with anybody for rational or wise reasons. And on the surface, you sounded like a horrible choice. An alcoholic homosexual who'd never had a mature relationship. But we could talk, and I felt like I could tell you anything, and in many senses we saved one another's lives, and it was the best choice I ever made.

WEEK 6, JUNE 1, 2019
Sylvia Plath (Kevin)

KK: How did you first hear about Sylvia Plath?

DB: I have no idea. I first got interested in her in the late '70s, when Janet, one of the first friends I made when I moved to San Francisco, gave me *Ariel* for my birthday. I wasn't expecting much, but I was blown away.

KK: In the late '70s she was already famous.

DB: She was famous as soon as she committed suicide. Successful before then, but not famous. Lately I've been astonished by how successful one can be in one's career yet not hit that ineffable height of being famous. Being famous is like having a totally recognizable brand, like one's work becomes a logo.

KK: I think it's one of the things that bonded us because I loved Sylvia Plath too, and you stood up for her in a hostile climate. And yet there were things about her that made me cringe, and you cringed at nothing. Your knowledge of Plath was much wider than mine. And you could actually quote passages from her, and if I tried, I would be grasping for straws, like, "Daddy, daddy, you are so dumb." That can't be in one of her poems.

DB: No, a dumb daddy wouldn't have as much power.

KK: As an evil one? I first heard about her from that article in *Time* magazine that detailed her suicide and the attempts to put Ariel into print, and that must have been the '60s. My parents didn't get *Time* magazine, but Professor Cassidy did, down the street, and there always was something in it about poetry. My god, I said to Catherine, my schoolmate in grade school, there's this guy called Frank O'Hara that got run over, not ten miles from here! And he's in *Time* magazine.

DB: Looking back, I'm amazed at how much, when we were kids, you could learn about poetry through the mass media. Like in *Time*—and I'm wondering why your parents didn't have a subscription, if it was too lowbrow or what. I talked my family into subscribing to the *Chicago Tribune*, just for its weekly book section, and there I learned about [Pablo] Neruda, for example. And I watched the 1966 series on the poets—Richard O. Moore's *USA: Poetry*—so I saw the Frank O'Hara episode, with its reenactment of him being hit by the dune buggy (or at least in my memory) and Anne Sexton playing lavish music to write her poems. All the incredible typewriters they sat at. I know I watched the whole series, but O'Hara and Sexton are who stuck.

KK: What broke the case for me was later in life when we got to meet Donald Allen and found out from him that employed by Time-Life was a fascinating woman called Rosalind Constable—hired by Henry Luce himself—exactly to put in these things and make people famous in the arts, often by death. The famous death of Jackson Pollock in a car crash—"death car girl" was driving the car and it crashed. All the famous things that happened in poetry were brainstorms of Rosalind Constable.

DB: What about somebody like Diane Wakoski—she, I imagine, made herself famous, like she'd be one of those blogging/tweeting poets these days who develops a career from the ground up.

KK: Or like that one Instagram poet with the two four-letter names—Rupi Kaur. She's the most famous poet in the world. And she's twenty-two.

DB: I never heard of her. I looked it up. She's twenty-six.

KK: How can you tell if she has actual institutional backing or if she just does this through fellow fans?

DB: If she didn't start out with institutional backing, I'm sure she has it now. That's the way capitalism works, via absorption.

KK: Did capitalism/absorption work for Sylvia? What did she have that nobody else had?

DB: In many ways, it worked against her. Plath is a genius, and she was turned into a cartoon. She worked incredibly hard to be successful and famous on her own terms—I'm thinking of her journals, where she rants about her jealousy of Adrienne Rich's success. But becoming a symbol of female rage and depression, that was so unfair. Male poets have been jumping off of bridges forever, and they don't have to bear that burden.

KK: For me, I believe if she had never gone to England, she never would have been famous. That it was just the moment.

DB: Hitching herself to Ted Hughes helped. She promoted him and boosted his career, and then she trailed along on his coattails.

KK: People must have been very jealous of her, the way that later on they got tired of Linda McCartney, another American heiress who came and captured another one of their princes of poetry, Paul McCartney.

DB: Plath wasn't an heiress. She was middle class, and after her father died of complications from diabetes, she was struggling middle class, raised by a single mother. Nothing glamorous about that. She had to create her own glamour. I never thought of people being jealous of her. Mostly you hear how selfish, moody, and bitchy she was. How dare she!

KK: And yet she rides on and on. No change in critical dictates have dethroned her, not entirely. At first people didn't like the way she threw Auschwitz around like it had happened to her and her heaping of all the great tragedies of twentieth-century history to make her heroines' domestic problems more intriguing, opening *The Bell Jar* the day the Rosenbergs were executed, for example. But she's still popular, and nobody remembers who the Rosenbergs were.

DB: I'd say that her point was that global trauma reverberates into our personal traumas. When the book opens, if I remember correctly, the heroine hasn't yet made her descent. The Rosenbergs were just setting the stage for how shitty America was at that point. Maybe we should write a novel and open it on the day Trump got elected.

KK: Or the day Freddie Gray got killed.

DB: We can all remember what we were doing when Kennedy got shot, or when the Twin Towers fell, so I like the idea of beginning something during a moment of shared trauma. All the divisiveness, and there are these moments where that falls away and the whole nation is suddenly tender together. Just a bleep.

KK: I remember when I first started teaching at California College of the Arts, it was maybe 2003, and yes, all of my students swore that nobody would ever forget what happened when the Twin Towers came down. Today, nobody knows and nobody really cares. I say, what do you all remember? And people like Andrew Durbin (under thirty) remember the Sandy Hook killings, and they remember Hurricane Sandy, and that's it.

DB: I was teaching Writers on Writing when 9/11 happened, and my first reader was Daphne Gottlieb, and she stood in front of the class and said how, after that, her writing felt meaningless and she was ashamed to be reading it, and she started crying. It was intense, but in a good way. It's like she was speaking the subconscious of the room.

KK: What impresses people about Sylvia is that she moved heaven and earth to go and live in England, where she became so unhappy she killed herself—and that you can't escape your past. And maybe all of us feel this way to some degree or another. She couldn't escape Adrienne Rich; she couldn't escape the porch that she crawled under to die when she was an undergrad; she couldn't escape Otto and the bees; or Smith College and feeling like a freak; and perhaps knowing that one day Gwyneth Paltrow would play her in the movies, and Blythe Danner would be Aurelia, that even her son would kill himself.

DB: She also had an amazing life; when things were good between her and Hughes, it sounded like poetry heaven, fantastically generative and exciting. One way I've related to Plath is that she really wasn't a rebel; she was always trying to be the best at any shitty social value, from toxic femininity to formalist poetry—but she could never really fit in. There were these deeper parts of herself that subverted her dronedom, and when that broke through at the end of her life, her poetry was unstoppable, the energy and innovation. I've always been willing to conform, but the part of me that can see what bullshit that is rebels every time. Thank god, or I'd have lived the most boring life, and I'd have stayed in relationships that would have destroyed my writing. Again, the suffering, for me, has been the biggest gift. I've sometimes felt that situations were against me, but more often than not, I can see how I was manipulating things so I'd be ousted from places that were toxic to me but that I couldn't get myself to leave. Do you relate to this pattern at all? You seem much less conformist from the get-go.

KK: I do believe that Plath outsmarted herself by having those children and swallowing that Kool-Aid, and she might well have known that that would lead to her death. Also England was on the cusp of glamour in 1963, when she died, but it was a hideous place for everybody but a very wealthy few.

DB: And it was the worst winter ever, and she was really sick and worried about money—and having to take care of these kids.

KK: And Assia calling her on the phone in that little Persian voice, saying, "Your man he belong to me now."

DB: Your version is a bit twisted, but what about my question above: do you personally relate to that pattern?

KK: I've almost gone to places that would have wrecked me, utterly, but some sense of preservation steered me away.

DB: Like what, for example?

KK: The thing I'm thinking of now is the subject of my new monograph. That is, how in the early days of AIDS, when none of us knew what a mammoth tragedy it would become, I stopped myself several times from making the kind of flip joke about AIDS that I later crucified Tom Clark and Ed Dorn for making. I was furious with them because it was so close. It might have been me who had given out to lesser poets the AIDS Award for Poetic Idiocy. This haunts me. Plath was only thirty when she died. She had the typical lifespan an AIDS patient would have had twenty years later. That's haunting too.

WEEK 7, JUNE 8, 2019
Now (Dodie)

Bruce Boone and ICU nurse visiting

DB: Kevin, what do you want to say to the world?

KK: I honestly thought that chemotherapy was not going to be a big deal. I thought I was going to have four or five sessions without any difficulty. Instead, after one session I wind up in a place where I don't know where I am, in grievous pain the likes of which I had never known—both mental and physical contusions.

BB: Kevin, you've always been so polite; you can't just say fuck you.

DB: Actually, since Kevin got sick he's said fuck you to many people. He's learned to be bitchy and not take any shit.

KK: In Redwood City they tried to move me to another room, a shared room—and I said to them, I am Kevin Killian, what you're doing is garbage.

DB: And it worked. Kevin got a fabulous private room where I could spend the night. You once said to me that you felt like if you'd been able to speak up for yourself more, you wouldn't have gotten sick.

KK: Yes, it's true. As I've come to view my life in the poetry world, I realize that the struggles of poetry led me into a hideous depression that wound up giving me cancer.

DB: But what about all the love in your world? You know you're a very loved person.

KK: I thought that the very poets who gave me cancer were the ones who loved me most.

DB: You're talking about a very small population, and one of your main pains in the ass, you were never close to. What about all the others who didn't hurt you?

KK: The Bard of Avon said it best, "They who have the power to hurt and do none, etc."

DB: Bruce, you've been around warring and disappointing poets since the '70s. How have you come to terms with that?

BB: At some point a few decades ago, I decided the poetry world was all fake and stopped.

DB: Kevin, what about all your artist friends?

KK: I love them because they bring in money.

BB: You set a high barrier.

DB: Let's get off the poetry scene.

KK: I'm at Kaiser in room 3212, and it's a dud. Not one good thing has happened here. Twelve hours of my hopes being washed away like soap bubbles barreling over a viscous basin. There's one work of art that intrigues me. It looks like a crucifix made of raw steel in some Spanish friar's chamber.

DB: What is that?

RN: It's a sling for lifting patients.

DB: What I've learned from all we've been through is how insanely generous the people we know are.

KK: Yes. I guess I'm feeling bitter.

Doctors arrive to insert Kevin's breathing tube.

JUNE 11, 2019

DB: I was going to write this in my journal, but my fountain pen has come apart and is all gunked up. Usually I can get it started again, but not tonight, which I took as a sign to write here instead. Hard to figure out what to do with this project, which you were so invested in and which we had so little time to work on. Before they put you on the breathing tube, you said, "We had a good long time together," and yes, we did, but not nearly enough. You could still come back for a bit, and I would love that more than anything, but nobody seems hopeful of that.

After dinner I returned to the hospital so I could spend some time alone with you. You looked peaceful, but when I held your hand, I couldn't feel your presence, like I have before. I held your left hand and thigh on and on but felt nothing, and I thought that perhaps you weren't as present as before, that you were leaving, and I told you that was alright, that you should do what you needed to do. I thought how your presence wasn't connected to your body, and I felt an assurance that that presence wouldn't leave me.

And then I felt a pulsing in your hand and thigh, and my hands began pulsing in synch with your pulsing, and I felt calm and my heart opened. It wasn't my love, but your love, which entered my heart. I said goodbye to you and drove home in a state of grace, my heart radiating love—your love in my core, radiating out from me.

Saturday night, when they put in the breathing tube and David Buuck and I spent the night at the hospital, I was exhausted, and I was able to get the night nurse to help me set up the one chair in the visitor's lounge that pulled out into a bed. You would have loved the nurse. She had tattoos down her arms and was very performance-y, dramatically announcing her every move in your room, as she changed and adjusted your medications. David and I fantasized she was a former exotic dancer.

As I lay in bed, I tried to imagine healing yellow light surrounding you and failed miserably. I was trying to force something that just wasn't there. Then I remembered the butterflies we wrote about here, and I saw a swarm of butterflies flickering around you, comforting you and sucking all the alien material out of your chest. And I could feel the butterflies doing the same for me, and I felt an intense connection between us, regardless of distance. I thought to myself—he may come out of this or he may not, and either is okay. I knew you were okay, and I felt at peace.

Since then, as I've held your hand, I've spoken to you about the butterflies, told you they were fluttering in your chest, healing and comforting. And I could feel your energy relax.

Dr. Strako called this morning. I guess she's been visiting you at the hospital the past couple of days. I asked her if she believed it helped to sit with you, and she said it definitely did help. She said on some level you knew I was there, and even if I sat and read a book, it helped, just my being there. She said you and I were among the special ten percent of her patients, meaning we were together for a long time and still loved each other—people who could be together for fifty years and still want to have breakfast together.

I know you sent me this love tonight; you sparked my heart so I wouldn't feel afraid. I will miss you so much, but I know you'll never leave me.

JUNE 13, 2019

DB: Even though your immune system collapsed today, they reduced your sedation. When Ariana Reines and Julian Brolaski visited, you smiled, despite the god-awful breathing tube, opening your eyes wide as if to allow all the good will in the world to beam out at them. I said, "Would you like Ariana to sing you a song?" and you nodded yes. Ariana sang Peter, Paul and Mary's "Autumn to May," with backup by Julian.

AR: Oh once I had a downey swan, she was so very frail
    She sat upon an oyster shell and hatched me out a snail
    The snail had changed into a bird, the bird to butterfly
    And he who tells a bigger tale would have to tell a lie.

DB: Tender butterfly, teller of tall tales, I love you.

THE STYLES
EILEEN
MYLES

DODIE
KEVIN
I'M IN
HEAVEN

Y'D

LOG

Notes

Dodie Bellamy's Crude Genius, by Megan Milks

1   Dodie Bellamy, *Barf Manifesto* (Brooklyn: Ugly Duckling Presse, 2008), 63.

2   Dodie Bellamy, "The Feminist Writers' Guild," in *When the Sick Rule the World* (South Pasadena, California: Semiotext(e), 2015), 87.

3   Dodie Bellamy, "Body Language," in *Academonia* (San Francisco: Krupskaya, 2006), 69.

4   Ibid., 75.

5   Ibid., 81.

6   Dodie Bellamy, *Pink Steam* (San Francisco: Suspect Thoughts Press, 2004), 22.

7   Dodie Bellamy, "The Fraud that is Eckankar: Hi Fubbi, this is Gakko," *San Diego Reader*, June 22, 1995.

8   Dodie Bellamy, "Cultured," in *The TV Sutras* (Brooklyn: Ugly Duckling Presse, 2014), 113.

9   Bellamy, "The Feminist Writers' Guild," in *When the Sick Rule the World*, 88.

10 Dodie Bellamy and Kevin Killian, eds., foreword to *Writers Who Love Too Much: New Narrative 1977–1997* (New York: Nightboat Books; Lebanon, New Hampshire: University Press of New England, 2017), I.

11 Bellamy and D'Allesandro's collaborative book *Real: The Letters of Mina Harker and Sam D'Allesandro* (Hoboken, New Jersey: Talisman House, Publishers, 1994), an offshoot of the project, was published six years after D'Allesandro's untimely death from AIDS.

12 Dodie Bellamy, *The Letters of Mina Harker* (West Stockbridge, Massachusetts: Hard Press, 1998), 16.

13 Bellamy, "The Cheese Stands Alone," in *Academonia*, 115.

14 Dodie Bellamy, *Cunt-Ups* (New York: Tender Buttons Press, 2001), 17.

15 Ariana Reines, in foreword to *Cunt Norton*, by Dodie Bellamy (Los Angeles: Les Figues Press, 2013).

16 The text from which Bellamy read is online at https://www.asu.edu/
pipercwcenter/how2journal/archive/online_archive/v2_1_2003/current/others/
bellamy.htm.

17 Dodie Bellamy, "Low Culture," in *Narrativity*, no. 3 (2003).

18 "About," *Belladodie*, accessed August 8, 2019, http://www.belladodie.com/about/.

19 Bellamy, "Digging Through Kathy Acker's Stuff," in *When the Sick Rule the
World*, 139.

20 Bellamy, "When the Sick Rule the World," in *When the Sick Rule the World*, 29.

21 Ibid., 30.

22 Ibid., 35.

23 Bellamy, "Cultured," in *The TV Sutras*, 106.

24 Bellamy, "Beyond Hunger," in *Academonia*, 104–105.

25 Bellamy, "In the Shadow of Twitter Towers," in *When the Sick Rule the World*, 196.

26 Ibid., 223.

Tiny Revolts, by Andrew Durbin

1 Derek Jarman and Olivia Laing, *Modern Nature: The Journals of Derek Jarman*
(London: Vintage, 2018).

2 Dodie Bellamy, *Cunt-Ups* (New York: Tender Buttons Press, 2001), 25.

3 Dodie Bellamy and Kevin Killian, eds., *Writers Who Love Too Much: New
Narrative Writing 1977–1997* (New York: Nightboat Books; Lebanon, New
Hampshire: University Press of New England, 2017), 265.

4 Bellamy and Killian, foreword to *Writers Who Love Too Much*, I.

5 Dennis Cooper, *Smothered in Hugs: Essays, Interviews, Feedback and Obituaries*
(New York: Harper Perennial, 2010), 68.

6 Robert Glück, *Communal Nude: Collected Essays* (South Pasadena, California:
Semiotext(e), 2016).

7 Bellamy and Killian, *Writers Who Love Too Much*, 266.

8 Dodie Bellamy, *the buddhist* (Portland, Oregon: Publication Studio, 2011), 127.

9 Dodie Bellamy, *Academonia* (San Francisco: Krupskaya, 2006), 42.

10 Bellamy and Killian, *Writers Who Love Too Much*, 266.

11 Dodie Bellamy, "The Beating of Our Hearts," in *When the Sick Rule the World* (South Pasadena, California: Semiotext(e), 2015), 160-180.

12 Ibid.

13 Georgina Colby, *Kathy Acker: Writing the Impossible* (Edinburgh, Scotland: Edinburgh University Press, 2016), 12.

14 Eileen Myles, "Everyday Barf," in *Sorry, Tree* (Seattle: Wave Books, 2007), 73-81.

15 Bellamy, "Barf Manifesto," in *When the Sick Rule the World*, 45.

16 Ibid.

17 Susan Signe Morrison, *Excrement in the Late Middle Ages: Sacred Filth and Chaucer's Fecopoetics* (New York: Palgrave Macmillan, 2008).

18 Bellamy, "Barf Manifesto," in *When the Sick Rule the World*, 63.

Reading Dodie Bellamy: Vulnerability and Vulgarity, by Kaye Mitchell

1 Elspeth Probyn, *Carnal Appetites: FoodSexIdentities* (London: Routledge, 2000), 3, 9.

2 Probyn claims that: "The moment of disgust that is produced by the encoding of bodies is geared to generating shame in the reader. From shame at one's feelings of disgust, these images sow the seeds of a more visceral accounting of difference, a bodily reaction to bodies." Ibid., 129. But she is really looking here at a very particular kind of disgust—at the body of the other—in a way that fails to take account of the broader experience and remit of disgust, e.g., its protective and/or hygienic function, its connection to dirt and disorder. She also assumes that we will feel shame at our disgust—when in fact it is more likely that we will feel (moral) superiority of some kind. In fact, it seems to me that what she is talking about is not really disgust, and that the self-disgust she touches on (the chapter opens with her averring that: "Like many, I spent much of my childhood feeling disgusting." Ibid., 127.) is really shame at bodily/ personal imperfection rather than disgust.

Probyn quotes Silvan Tomkins's view on disgust, that it has "evolved to protect the human being from coming too close." Silvan Tomkins, *Affect, Imagery, Consciousness*, vol. III (New York: Springer, 1991), 15. She suggests that: "Shame, on the other hand, is in part generated by the recognition of having been too close, where proximity to the other has been terminated." Probyn, *Carnal Appetites*, 133. Again, this is rather too neat an opposition—what Tomkins calls "interest" is not quite the same as "proximity." She suggests that "if taste is socially and historically constructed, then so too must extreme distaste and disgust [*sic*]," but it doesn't follow that if taste is socially constructed, disgust must be too; arguably there are varieties of disgust that are social and varieties that are biological. When Probyn asks why "disgust feel[s] simultaneously so primal and so social," the answer is simply: because it is both! Or perhaps: because there are different varieties of disgust. Her attempts to present disgust and shame as "distinct yet doubled" are interesting but tend to result in reductive definitions of each in order to show them as "doubled." Ibid.

3   Probyn, *Carnal Appetites*, 134.

4   "About," *Belladodie*, accessed August 8, 2019, http://www.belladodie.com/about/.

5   Dodie Bellamy, "Low Culture: Sex/Body/Writing," in Mary Burger, Robert Glück, Camille Roy, and Gail Scott, eds., *Biting the Error: Writers Explore Narrative* (Toronto: Coach House Books, 2004), 235, 234.

6   Dodie Bellamy, *Academonia* (San Francisco: Krupskaya, 2006), 126.

7   Silvan Tomkins, "Shame-Humiliation and Contempt-Disgust," in Eve Kosofsky Sedgwick and Adam Frank, eds., *Shame and Its Sisters* (Durham: Duke University Press, 1995), 137.

8   Sandra Bartky, *Femininity and Domination* (London: Routledge, 1990), 93.

9   Ibid., 84.

10 Ibid., 85. As Bartky explains in a footnote, Husseen Abdilahi Bulhan, in *Frantz Fanon and the Psychology of Oppression* (New York: Plenum Press, 1985), "characterizes a 'generalized condition of dishonor' as a status in which one's person lacks integrity, worth and autonomy and in which one is subject to violations of space, time, energy, mobility, bonding and identity." Ibid., 133n6.

11 Bartky, *Femininity and Domination*, 95.

12 Bellamy, *Academonia*, 126.

13 Giorgio Agamben, *Remnants of Auschwitz*, trans. Daniel Heller-Roazen (New York: Zone Books, 2002), 107. My emphasis in second quotation.

14   Peter Stallybrass and Allon White, *The Politics and Poetics of Transgression* (Ithaca: Cornell University Press, 1986), 3.

15 Ibid., 4-5.

16 Christopher Breu, "Disinterring the real: Dodie Bellamy's *The Letters of Mina Harker* and the late-capitalist literature of materiality," *Textual Practice* 26, no. 2 (2012): 266.

17 Ibid., 267.

18 Ibid., 268, 271.

19 Eve Kosofsky Sedgwick describes shame as "both peculiarly contagious and peculiarly individuating." See her article "Queer Performativity: Henry James's *The Art of the Novel*," *GLQ* 1, no. 1 (November 1993): 5.

20 Sarah Todd, "An Interview with Dodie Bellamy," *Girls Like Giants* (blog), April 172012, https://girlslikegiants.wordpress.com/2012/04/17/an-interview-with-dodie-bellamy/.

21 Trans. Marjorie Perloff, in Marjorie Perloff, *Unoriginal Genius: Poetry by Other Means in the New Century* (Chicago: University of Chicago Press, 2010), 3–4.

22 Jennifer Cooke, review of *Cunt-Ups* by Dodie Bellamy, *Hix Eros Poetry Review* 5 (September 2014): 8.

23 Sara Wintz, "From Cut-Up to *Cunt Up*: Dodie Bellamy in Conversation," *Harriet* (blog), The Poetry Foundation, November 21, 2013.

24 Dodie Bellamy, "Statement," in Caroline Bergvall, Laynie Browne, Teresa Carmody, and Vanessa Place, eds., *I'll Drown My Book: Conceptual Writing by Women* (Los Angeles: Les Figues Press, 2012), 339.

25 Bellamy, *Academonia*, 75.

26 Bellamy, "Low Culture," in *Biting the Error*, 232.

27 Cooke, review of *Cunt-Ups* by Dodie Bellamy, 9–10.

28 Elspeth Probyn, *Blush: Faces of Shame* (Minneapolis: University of Minnesota Press, 2005), xvii.

29 Dodie Bellamy, *Cunt-Ups* [2001] (New York City: Tender Buttons, 2018), 26.

30 Bellamy, *Cunt-Ups*, 50.

31 Bellamy, *Cunt-Ups*, 72.

32 Bellamy, *Cunt-Ups*, 38.

33 Bellamy, "Statement," in *I'll Drown My Book*, 338.

34 Bellamy, *Cunt-Ups*, 69–70.

35 Bellamy, *Cunt-Ups*, 24.

36 Bellamy, *Cunt-Ups*, 25.

37 Bellamy, *Cunt-Ups*, 26.

38 Bellamy, *Cunt-Ups*, 49.

39 Note that this is perhaps even more strikingly the case in Bellamy's later *Cunt Norton* (Los Angeles: Les Figues Press, 2013), in which canonical poetry by the likes of Shakespeare, Tennyson, Yeats, and others, taken from the culturally revered *Norton Anthology of Poetry*, is spliced with Bellamy's pornographic narrative; the masculine canon (Emily Dickinson is the only female poet to be "cunted" here) is thus violated by Bellamy's crude language and irreverent, penetrative desire. As Ariana Reines comments, in her foreword to *Cunt Norton*: "Shakespeare is commended to his or their proper androgyny . . . . In this book, Ginsberg is better and gayer than Ginsberg. . . . To take the bracing,

medicinal Burroughsian cut as far as Dodie Bellamy takes it, such that it both cuts and makes to pour forth, means to render each cut into true congress: to cunt means to mark the spot where rupture and fusion become indivisible."

40 David Banash, "The History and Practice of Cut-Ups," *American Book Review* 32, no. 6 (2011): 10.

41 Bellamy, "Low Culture," in *Biting the Error*, 232.

42 Edward S. Robinson, *Shift Linguals: Cut-Up Narratives from William S. Burroughs to the Present* (Amsterdam: Rodopi, 2011), 43.

43 In early works such as 1972's *The Burning Bombing of America* and 1973's *Rip-Off Red, Girl Detective* (published together, New York: Grove Press, 2002), Acker makes use of Burroughs-style cut-up, incorporating passages from other works. Her work then shifts, according to Edward S. Robinson's reading, "from syntactic cut-ups toward outright plagiarism and a method that could be more accurately described as cut and paste than cut-up." Robinson, *Shift Linguals*, 154. In such works as 1973's *The Childlike Life of the Black Tarantula by the Black Tarantula* (New York: TVRT Press, 1978) and 1975's *The Adult Life of Toulouse Lautrec by Henri Toulouse Lautrec* (New York: TVRT Press, 1978), "Acker intercut larger sections of narrative from different sources. Where she overtly plagiarized from her source texts, by simply copying sections of them out, she sought to 'represent' the texts, and address the question, 'if I repeated the same text, would it be the same text?'" Robinson, *Shift Linguals*, 154.

44 See, for example: Susan Bordo, *Unbearable Weight: Feminism, Western Culture, and the Body* (Berkeley: University of California Press, 2004); Avril Horner and Angela Keane, eds., *Body Matters: Feminism, Textuality, Corporeality* (Manchester, United Kingdom: Manchester University Press, 2000); Janet Price and Margrit Shildrik, eds., *Feminist Theory and the Body: A Reader* (New York: Routledge, 1999).

45 Cooke, review of *Cunt-Ups* by Dodie Bellamy, 10.

46 Bellamy, *Cunt-Ups*, 66.

47 Andrew Ketcham, review of *Cunt Norton* by Dodie Bellamy, *New Orleans Review*, 2014, http://www.neworleansreview.org/cunt-norton/.

48 Dodie Bellamy, *the buddhist* (Portland, Oregon: Publication Studio, 2011), 42.

49 Bellamy, *Academonia*, 74–75.

50 Bellamy, *Cunt-Ups*, 20.

51 Bellamy, "Low Culture," in *Biting the Error*, 232.

52 Bellamy, *Cunt-Ups*, 28.

53 Bellamy, *the buddhist*, 84.

54 Todd, "An Interview with Dodie Bellamy," *Girls Like Giants* (blog).

55 Bellamy, *the buddhist*, 37, 49.

56 Ibid., 34–35, 42.

57 Sara Ahmed, "Interview with Judith Butler," *Sexualities* 19, no. 4 (2016): 485.

58 Judith Butler, *Undoing Gender* (London: Routledge, 2004), 30.

59 George Shulman, "On Vulnerability as Judith Butler's Language of Politics: From 'Excitable Speech' to 'Precarious Life,'" *Women's Studies Quarterly* 39, nos. 1–2 (2011): 232.

60 From the press release for the exhibition at Paula Cooper Gallery, New York (April 9–June 6, 2009): "Calle orchestrates a virtual chorus of women's interpretations and assessments of a breakup letter she received in an email. In photographic portraits, textual analysis, and filmed performances, the show presents a seemingly exhaustive compendium with contributions ranging from a clairvoyant's response to a scientific study, a children's fairytale to a Talmudic exegesis, among many others. Examining the conditions and possibilities of human emotions, *Take Care of Yourself* opens up ideas about love and heartache, gender and intimacy, labor and identity."

61 Anna Watkins Fisher, "Manic Impositions: The Parasitical Art of Chris Kraus and Sophie Calle," *WSQ: Women's Studies Quarterly* 40, nos. 1–2 (2012): 223-224.

62 Todd, "Interview with Dodie Bellamy," *Girls Like Giants* (blog).

63 Bellamy, *the buddhist*, 89.

64 Quoted in Amelia Jones, *Body Art / Performing the Subject* (Minneapolis: University of Minnesota Press, 1998), 3.

65 Bellamy, *Academonia*, 115.

66 Bellamy, *the buddhist*, 89.

67 Bellamy, *Academonia*, 126.

68 Bellamy, *the buddhist*, 143.

69 Ibid., 144.

70 For comparison, see how Susan Bordo reads "images of unwanted bulges and erupting stomachs" as "a metaphor for anxiety about internal processes out of control—uncontained desire, unrestrained hunger, uncontrolled impulse." Bordo, *Unbearable Weight*, 189.

71 Bellamy, *the buddhist*, 13.

72 Ibid., 12, 34.

73 Ibid., 29.

74 Ibid., 35.

75 Ibid., 34–35.

76 Bellamy, *Academonia*, 51.

77 Todd, "An Interview with Dodie Bellamy," *Girls Like Giants* (blog).

78 Bellamy, "Statement," in *I'll Drown My Book*, 338.

79 Kaye Mitchell, "Introduction: The Gender Politics of Experiment," *Contemporary Women's Writing* 9, no. 1 (2015): 1–15.

80 Jennifer Ashton, "Our Bodies, Our Poems," *American Literary History* 19, no. 1 (2007): 211–231 (214); Jennifer Scappettone, "Bachelorettes, Even: Strategic Embodiment in Contemporary Experimentalism by Women," *Modern Philology* 105, no. 1 (2007): 180–181.

81 Bellamy, *Academonia*, 81–82.

82 Bellamy, *the buddhist*, 85–86.

83 Ibid., 44.

84 Ibid., 73.

85 Ibid., 111.

86 Ibid., 108.

87 Ibid., 130.

88 Ibid., 70.

89 Christopher Higgs, "Colonized on Every Level: An Interview with Dodie Bellamy," *The Paris Review*, July 29, 2014. The choice of "mortified" is an interesting one on Bellamy's part; "mortification" can mean both "great embarrassment and shame," and "the action of subduing one's bodily desires" (i.e., "mortification of the flesh")—something that Bellamy notably refuses to do.

90 Bellamy, "Low Culture," in *Biting the Error*, 226.

91 Probyn, *Carnal Appetites*, 9, 134.

92 An earlier version of this essay appeared as a chapter, with the title "Vulnerability and Vulgarity: The Uses of Shame in the Work of Dodie Bellamy," in Barry Sheils and Julie Walsh, eds., *Shame and Modern Writing* (New York: Routledge, 2018), 165–185.

Bibliography

BOOKS

Cunt-Ups. Reprinted with introduction by Sophie Robinson. New York: Tender Buttons Press, 2019.

Writers Who Love Too Much: New Narrative 1977–1997. Edited with Kevin Killian. New York: Nightboat Books; Lebanon, New Hampshire: University Press of New England, 2017.

When the Sick Rule the World. South Pasadena, California: Semiotext(e), 2015.

The TV Sutras. Brooklyn: Ugly Duckling Presse, 2014.

Cunt Norton. Los Angeles: Les Figues Press, 2013.

the buddhist. New York: Emily Books, 2012. E-book.

the buddhist. Portland, Oregon: Publication Studio, 2011.

Academonia. San Francisco: Krupskaya, 2006.

> **Need the success of a political group be measured on its impact on a larger social order? What about the ways it transforms the lives and psyches of its members—these tiny revolts—are they not profound?**
>
> ("The Feminist Writers' Guild," 2015)

The Letters of Mina Harker. Reprinted with introduction by Dennis Cooper. Madison, Wisconsin: University of Wisconsin Press, 2004.

Pink Steam. San Francisco: Suspect Thoughts Press, 2004.

Cunt-Ups. New York: Tender Buttons Press, 2001.

The Letters of Mina Harker. West Stockbridge, Massachusetts: Hard Press, 1998.

Real: The Letters of Mina Harker and Sam D'Allesandro. With Sam D'Allesandro. Hoboken, New Jersey: Talisman House, Publishers, 1994.

Feminine Hijinx. New York: Hanuman Books, 1990.

CHAPBOOKS

More Important than the Object. In *Say Bye to Reason and Hi to Everything*, edited by Andrew Durbin. New York: Capricious, 2016. Box set of five chapbooks.

Daphne's Game. Published in conjunction with *Transiting Desire*, an exhibition at She Works Flexible, Houston, June 26–September 11, 2015.

The Beating of Our Hearts. South Pasadena, California: Semiotext(e), 2014. Published in conjunction with the Whitney Biennial 2014, Whitney Museum of American Art, New York, March 7–May 25, 2014.

Whistle While You Dixie. Los Angeles: Susan Silton, 2010.

Barf Manifesto. Brooklyn: Ugly Duckling Presse, 2008.

Mother Montage. Brooklyn: Belladonna Books, 2008.

The Bandaged Lady. Published in conjunction with *Hanging Matters*, an exhibition of work by Tariq Alvi at [2nd floor projects], San Francisco, March 8–April 13, 2008.

Fat Chance. Vancouver, British Columbia: Nomados, 2003.

Hallucinations. Buffalo, New York: Meow Press, 1997.

Broken English. With Roberto Harrison. Buffalo, New York: Meow Press, 1996.

Answer. Buffalo, New York: Leave Books, 1993.

The Debbies I Have Known. San Francisco: e.g. Press, 1983.

WORKS IN ANTHOLOGIES AND CATALOGUES

"Bee Reaved." Published in conjunction with *The Making of Husbands*, a Christina Ramberg exhibition at KW Institute for Contemporary Art, Berlin, September 14, 2019–January 5, 2020.

> **When the sick rule the world, perfume will be outlawed.**
>
> **("When the Sick Rule the World," 2012)**

Catalogue essay. With Kevin Killian. In *Mike Kelley: Pushing and Pulling, Pulling and Pushing*. San Francisco: Colpa Books, 2019. Published in conjunction with an exhibition of the same title at 500 Capp Street, San Francisco, November 3, 2018–February 16, 2019.

"Boobs." In *Legsicon*. London: Book Works, 2019. Published in conjunction with *LAURE PROUVOST: AM-BIG-YOU-US LEGSICON* at M HKA, Antwerp, February 8–May 19, 2019.

"The Violence of the Image." Published in conjunction with *Henrik Olesen*, Museo Nacional Centro de Arte Reina Sofía, Madrid, June 26–October 21, 2019.

"The Kingdom of Isolation." In *Hello Leonora, Soy Anne Walsh*, ed. Rachel Churner. San Francisco: no place press, 2019. Published in conjunction with *They*, a solo exhibit by Anne Walsh at the Luggage Store, San Francisco, February 2017.

"Attack of the Shiny Black Oxford." In *Small Blows Against Encroaching Totalitarianism*, Volume One, The Manifesto Series. San Francisco: McSweeney's Books, 2018.

"Hoarding as Écriture." In *Ways of Re-Thinking Literature*, edited by Tom Bishop and Donatien Grau. London; New York: Routledge, 2018.

> **Sex can't be reduced to events that happen to a person. Sex is a trap, a labyrinth, a matrix that engulfs you. There's no way out. If I were to write the story of my life with emotional honesty, my relationship to my body would be the most important thing.**
>
> **("Low Culture," 2003)**

"Laugh and Cry: A Conversation between Dodie Bellamy and Kevin Killian." With Kevin Killian. In *Ugo Rondinone: the world just makes me laugh*. Milan, Italy: Mousse Publishing, 2017. Published in conjunction with an exhibition of the same title, University of California, Berkeley Art Museum, June 29–August 26, 2017.

"Emptied Out." In *I Love John Giorno*, edited by Laura Hoptman and Mónica de la Torre. *The Brooklyn Rail*, July 1, 2017. Published in conjunction with *Ugo Rondinone: I Love John Giorno*, an exhibition held at multiple venues, New York, June 2017.

"Cinderella Syndrome: after Ellen Cantor." In *Ellen Cantor: A History of the World as it Became Known to Me*. San Francisco: CCA Wattis Institute; Berlin: Sternberg Press; Künstlerhaus Stuttgart; New York: PARTICIPANT INC., 2018. Published in conjunction with *Ellen Cantor: Cinderella Syndrome*, an exhibition at CCA Wattis Institute for Contemporary Arts, San Francisco, December 8, 2015–February 10, 2016, and Künstlerhaus Stuttgart, Germany, April 2–July 31, 2016.

"Hans Bellmer." In *San Francisco Museum of Modern Art 360°: Views on the Collection*, edited by Judy Bloch and Suzanne Stein. San Francisco: San Francisco Museum of Modern Art, 2016.

Cunt-Ups. In *Tender Omnibus*. New York: Tender Buttons Press, 2016.

"Cunt Wordsworth." In *BAX 2015: Best American Experimental Writing*, edited by Seth Abramson, Jesse Damiani, and Douglas Kearney. Middletown, Connecticut: Wesleyan University Press, 2015.

"These Lips Which Are Not One." In *TrenchArt Monographs: Hurry Up Please Its Time*, edited by Teresa Carmody and Vanessa Place. Los Angeles: Les Figues Press, 2015.

"Outside the As-Is." In *Night Begins the Day*, edited by Renny Pritikin and Lily Siegel. Published in conjunction with *Night Begins the Day: Rethinking Space, Time, and Beauty*, an exhibition at the Contemporary Jewish Museum, San Francisco, June 18–September 20, 2015.

"Cunt Chaucer." In *The Animated Reader: Poetry of Surround Audience*, edited by Brian Droitcour. New York: New Museum and McNally Jackson, 2015. Published in conjunction with *Surround Audience*, the New Museum 2015 Triennial, New York, February 25–May 24, 2015.

"Writing Experiments." In *Please Add This to the List: Teaching Bernadette Mayer's Sonnets & Experiments*, edited by Katy Bohinc and Lee Ann Brown. New York: Tender Buttons Press, 2014.

"The Center of Gravity." In *Field Work*, edited by Kevin Killian and Frank Smigiel. San Francisco: San Francisco Museum of Modern Art, 2013. Published in conjunction with *Mark di Suvero at Crissy Field*, an outdoor installation, San Francisco, May 22, 2013–May 26, 2014.

"I Must Not Forget What I Already Know." Presented at Southern Exposure, San Francisco, May 30, 2013. Written in response to *Reverse Rehearsals*, an exhibition at Southern Exposure, May 7–June 1, 2013.

Introduction to *Lost Treasures from Bay Area Art Archives*. Presented in conjunction with screening of *The Blue Tape*, by Kathy Acker and Alan Sondheim, at The Lost Church, San Francisco, May 7, 2013.

> I don't just love, I absorb people and everybody suffers. This is why I've become so rigid.
> (*The TV Sutras*, 2014)

"The Beating of Our Hearts." Published in conjunction with *See Red Women's Workshop*, an exhibition at the Institute for Contemporary Arts, London, December 5, 2012–January 13, 2013.

"Blanche and Stanley" and "Crimes Against Genre." In *Revolution: An Annotated Reader*, edited by Lisa Robertson and Matthew Stadler. Portland, Oregon: Publication Studio, 2012.

"Cunt-Ups." In *I'll Drown My Book: Conceptual Writing By Women*, edited by Caroline Bergvall, Laynie Browne, Teresa Carmody, and Vanessa Place. Los Angeles: Les Figues Press, 2012.

"Here Comes the Bride/Groom." With Kevin Killian. In *The Air We Breathe: Artists and Poets Reflect on Gay Marriage Equality*, edited by Apsara DiQuinzio. Published in conjunction with *The Air We Breathe*, an exhibition at the San Francisco Museum of Modern Art, November 5, 2011–February 20, 2012.

"July 4, 2011." In *Conversations at the Wartime Cafe: A Decade of War 2001–2011*, edited by Sean Manzano. Berkeley: CreateSpace, 2011.

"Phone Home." In *Life as We Show It*, edited by Brian Pera and Masha Tupitsyn. San Francisco: City Lights Publishers, 2009.

"Dogs Without a Face." In *Mythtym*, edited by Trinie Dalton. New York: PictureBox, 2008.

> **Gravity does not bend. Art writers lie. Art lies. It was the lie of art I wanted more than anything else as a child.**
>
> ("The Center of Gravity," 2013)

"Snowglobe." In *Good Times Bad Trips*, edited by Cliff Hengst and Scott Hewicker. Published in conjunction with *S.A.N.E. (Something/Anything/Nothing/Everything)*, an exhibition of work by Cliff Hengst and Scott Hewicker at Gallery 16, San Francisco, September 14–November 3, 2007.

"Digging through Kathy Acker's Stuff." In *The Back Room, An Anthology*, edited by Matthew Stadler. Portland, Oregon: Clear Cut Press, 2007.

"Tenebrae." With Kevin Killian. In *Saints of Hysteria: A Half-Century of Collaborative American Poetry*. New York: Soft Skull Press, 2007.

"Blue Screen." In *Bay Poetics*, edited by Stephanie Young. Cambridge, Massachusetts: Faux Press, 2006.

"Digression as Power: Dennis Cooper and the Aesthetics of Distance." In *Enter at Your Own Risk: The Dangerous Art of Dennis Cooper*, edited by Leora Lev. Madison, Wisconsin: Fairleigh Dickinson University Press, 2006.

"Undeath of the Author" and "Savage Magic." In *Séance*, edited by Christine Wertheim and Matias Viegener. Los Angeles: Make Now Press, 2006.

"Low Culture: Sex/Body/Writing." In *Biting the Error: Writers Explore Narrative*, edited by Mary Burger, Robert Glück, Camille Roy, and Gail Scott. Toronto: Coach House Books, 2004.

"Aaron's Mix." In *Mix Tape: The Art of Cassette Culture*, edited by Thurston Moore. New York: Universe, 2004.

"Savage Magic: for Matt Greene." In *The Dogs*, edited by Casey McKinney. Published in conjunction with *The Dogs*, an exhibition at Karyn Lovegrove Gallery, Los Angeles, July 2004.

"Spew Forth." In *Frozen Tears*, edited by John Russell. Birmingham, United Kingdom: ARTicle Press, 2004.

"Sexspace." In *Bottoms Up*, edited by Diana Cage. New York: Soft Skull Press, 2004.

"Phonezone." In *Pills, Thrills, Chills, and Heartache: Adventures in the First Person*, edited by Clint Catalyst and Michelle Tea. Los Angeles: Alyson Publications, 2004.

Excerpt from "Fat Chance." In *The Big Book of Erotic Ghost Stories*, edited by Greg Wharton. New York: Bookspan, 2004.

"Can You Hear Me Major Tom." In *Fascination: The Bowie Show*. Published in conjunction with an exhibition of the same title at Gallery 16, San Francisco, August 2002.

Excerpt from "Fat Chance." In *Technologies of Measure: A Celebration of Bay Area Women Writers*, edited by Kate Colby, Rena Rosenwasser, and Elizabeth Treadwell Jackson. San Francisco: Small Press Traffic Literary Arts Center, 2002. Published in conjunction with the F-Word festival, San Francisco, 2002.

"Cracks in the Ceiling." In *Dirty Words*, edited by Casey McKinney. Published in conjunction with *Dirty Deeds Done Dirt Cheap*, an exhibition at the Atlanta Contemporary Art Center, September 2001.

"Spew Forth." In *Best American Erotica 2001*, edited by Susie Bright. New York: Simon and Schuster, 2001.

"Cunt-Up #15." In *The Blind See Only this World: Poems for John Wieners*, edited by William Corbett, Michael Gizzi, and Joseph Torra. New York: Granary Books; Boston: Pressed Wafer, 2000.

"He sucked the marrow from me." In *Physics for Buddhists*. Boulder, Colorado: Kavyayantra Press, 1999.

> **Breaking her diet with a huge slice of German chocolate cake, Lizzie asks, "Doesn't the word 'complicity' sound like a woman's name." I smile and steal a bite.**
>
> ("Complicity," 1988)

"Hot Tub." In *Lodger*, edited by Glen Helfand. Published in conjunction with *Sap: the Residue of the San Francisco Art Scene*, an exhibition at the Lanai Motel, San Francisco, October 1998.

"You Edju." Published in conjunction with *Bottoms Up*, an exhibition at The Lab, San Francisco, June 1998.

Excerpt from *The Letters of Mina Harker* and "Delinquent." In *Moving Borders: Three Decades of Innovative Writing by Women*, edited by Mary Margaret Sloan. Hoboken, New Jersey: Talisman House, Publishers, 1998.

Trans. "on my desk." By Sabine Macher. In *Twenty-Two New (to North America) French Writers*, in *Raddle Moon* 16, edited by Norma Cole and Stacy Doris. Vancouver, British Columbia: Kootenay School of Writing, 1997.

Excerpt from *Real: The Letters of Mina Harker and Sam D'Allesandro*. In *Particular Voices: Portraits of Gay and Lesbian Writers*, edited by Robert Giard. Cambridge, Massachusetts: MIT Press, 1997.

Excerpt from *The Letters of Mina Harker*. In *Primary Trouble: An Anthology of Contemporary American Poetry*, edited by Joseph Donahue, Edward Foster, and Leonard Schwartz. Hoboken, New Jersey: Talisman House, Publishers, 1996.

> **My karma ran over my dogma.**
> (*The Letters of Mina Harker*, 1998)

Excerpt from "Broken English." In *Millennium Coming: The New Degenerate Art Show*. Published in conjunction with an exhibition of the same title at The Lab, San Francisco, October–November, 1995.

"Hot." In *Wildside*, an exhibition at Los Angeles Contemporary Exhibitions, September 21, 1995.

"Broken English." In *Smells Like Vinyl*, an exhibition at Roger Merians Gallery, New York, July 6–August 18, 1995.

"Yoko Piece." In *This Is Not Her*. Published in conjunction with *PIECE! 9 Artists Consider Yoko Ono*, an exhibition at Kiki Gallery, San Francisco, February 1995.

"Dear Laurie." In *The New Fuck You: Adventures in Lesbian Reading*, edited by Liz Kotz and Eileen Myles. New York: Semiotext(e), 1995.

Essay on G. B. Jones. In *Farm 7 / The Gentlewomen of California* 8 (copublication). New York: Feature and Instituting Contemporary Idea, 1995.

"Punctured." In *His Bride*, edited by D. L. Alvarez. Published in conjunction with *Tiny Shoes*, an exhibition at New Langton Arts, San Francisco, 1994.

"Delinquent." In *A Poetics of Criticism*, edited by Kristin Prevallet, Pam Rehm, Juliana Spahr, and Mark Wallace. Buffalo, New York: Leave Books, 1994.

"Dear Cassandra." In *The Art of Practice: 45 Contemporary Poets*, edited by Dennis Barone and Peter Ganick. Elmwood, Connecticut: Potes & Poets Press, 1994.

"Dear Quincey." In *Exhausted Autumn*, edited by Richard Hawkins. Published in conjunction with *Sweet Oleander: An Exhibition of Works by Tony Greene*, an exhibition at Los Angeles Contemporary Exhibitions, 1991.

"Dear Dennis." In *High Risk*, edited by Amy Scholder and Ira Silverberg. New York: Plume, 1991.

"Mishmashing." In *Patterns/Contexts/Time: A Symposium on Contemporary Poetry*, edited by Phillip Foss and Charles Bernstein. *Tyuonyi* 6/7. Santa Fe, New Mexico: Recursos de Santa Fe, 1990.

"Complicity." In *Semiotext(e) USA*. New York: Semiotext(e), 1988.

"No Live Organism Can Continue for Long to Exist Sanely Under Conditions of Absolute Reality / An Experience of Chantal Akerman's Jeanne Dielman, 23 Quai du Commerce, 1080 Bruxelles." In *New Critical Perspectives*, edited by Bruce Boone. *Soup* 4. San Francisco: Steve Abbott, 1985.

FICTION/MEMOIR/POETRY IN MAGAZINES

> **These are the things that are wrong with me. I'm a woman. I write about sex. I'm too old, I'm too weird. I'm white. I'm a white woman who's too old to write about sex.**
>
> **(*Academonia*, 2006)**

"Photo Op: Dodie Bellamy on the compulsion to document." *Artforum.com*, May 14, 2019.

"The Ghosts We Live With." *Los Angeles Review of Books*, No. 22: Occult, 2019.

"On History and Endurance." *Art Practical*, March 20, 2019. Part of their Living and Working Series, funded by the California Arts Council.

"I Heart You: Dodie Bellamy on Valentine's Day." *Artforum.com*, February 14, 2019.

"The Return of Inanna: Dodie Bellamy on becoming undone." *Artforum.com*, January 4, 2019.

"Leaky Boundaries: Dodie Bellamy on her European travels." *Artforum.com*, December 2, 2018.

"The Violence of the Image." *11-11,* Fall 2018.

"Cunt DADA." *Cabaret Wittgenstein: Laboratory for Anti-Dystopian Writing*, curated by Ricardo Domeneck, May 16, 2016.

"Ephemeral." *Open Space* (blog). San Francisco Museum of Modern Art, November 9, 2015.

"Digging Through Kathy Acker's Stuff." *Literary Hub*, November 6, 2015.

"These Lips Which Are Not One," "Cunt Wordsworth," "Cunt Olson." *PEN Poetry Series*, February 21, 2014.

"Cunt Norton," "Cunt Blake," "Cunt Dickinson," "Cunt Crane." *Maggy*, no. 5 (February 2014).

"Cunt Milton." *Night Papers* VI (2014).

"The Feraltern." *ON Contemporary Practice*, 2014.

"When the Sick Rule the World." *Bombay Gin* 38, no. 1 (2012).

"Rascal Guru." *The Swan's Rag*, no. 4 (August 2011).

"Girl Body." *Action Yes Quarterly* 1, no. 12 (Winter 2010).

"Turn On the Heat." *News of Common Possibility*, no. 2 (December 2009).

"Rearview." *Court Green* 6 (2009).

"Ladies Who Poetry." *Abraham Lincoln* 3 (Summer/Fall 2008).

Excerpt from "Phone Home." *Apothecary*: "Ether," July 11, 2008.

Excerpt from "Mere Life." *Big Bell*, no. 1 (Spring 2008).

"Lady Jane." *Mandorla*, no. 9 (2006).

"Blanche and Stanley." *Hot Whiskey*, no. 2 (2006).

"Dogs without a Face." *Werewolf Express*, edited by Trinie Dalton. Published in conjunction with *The Zine Unbound: Kults, Werewolves, and Sarcastic Hippies*, an exhibition at Yerba Buena Center for the Arts, San Francisco, October 7– December 30, 2005.

"Peering." *Instant City*, no. 2 (Fall 2005).

"Monica." *Jouissance*, no. 1 (Fall 2005).

"Trouble Man." *San Diego Reader*, August 11, 2005.

Excerpt from "Fat Chance." *Court Green*, no. 1 (2004).

"Fat Chance." In "Inappropriated Others," edited by Jeanne Heuving. *HOW2* 2, no. 1 (Spring 2003).

"In Dutch." *Bombay Gin*, no. 29 (2003).

"Ampersand." *Ecopoetics*, no. 2 (Fall 2002).

Excerpt from "Fat Chance." *Matrix*, no. 62 (Fall 2002).

"Round Robin." With Stephen Beachy, C. Bard Cole, Dennis Cooper, Mark Ewert, Phoebe Gloeckner, Kevin Killian, Casey McKinney, Douglas Martin, Brian Pera, Ira Sachs, and Teresa Theophano. *Low Blue Flame*, no. 4 (2002).

"They Spruce Themselves Up" and "There Is Plenty to Suck." *Near South*, no. 2 (Fall 2002).

"Another Sexual Act." *PomPom*, no. 2 (April 2002).

"Post-It." *Shampoo*, no. 11 (April 2002).

> **Whistle, whistle, you ain't getting to me, bitch. The whistle is the piercing blade of rationality.**
>
> ("Whistle While You Dixie," 2010)

"Ampersand." *Salt Hill*, no. 12 (Spring 2002).

"To Cut #1." *Old Gold*, no. 1 (March 2002).

"Cunt-Ups #18–20." *Stretcher*, no. 2 (February 2002).

"First Time" and excerpt from "Fat Chance." *nocturnes* (Oakland, California) 2 (Winter 2002).

"Cunt-Ups #17–18." *Open City*, no. 14 (Winter 2001–2002).

"Cracks in the Ceiling." *Mark(s) Quarterly of the Arts* 2, no. 3 (December 2001).

"Cunt-Ups #10–12." *HOW2* 1, no. 5 (March 2001).

"Everything Seen Through the Lens of Over." August Press Broadside Series, 2001.

"Cunt-Up #21." *Can We Have Our Ball Back*, November 2000.

"Cunt-Ups #5–7." *Chain* 7: "Memoir/Anti-Memoir" (Summer 2000).

"Cunt-Ups #13–14." *Kenning*, no. 10 (Spring 2000).

"Cunt-Ups #5–8." *West Coast Line* 31 (Spring 2000).

"Touch." *Primary Writing*, no. 22 (February 2000).

"Cunt-Ups #1–4." *San Jose Manual of Style*, Winter 2000.

"Letterwriting Assignment 1: Tell Somebody Something You've Always Wanted to Tell Them" and "Letterwriting Assignment 2: Follow Bernadette's Instructions." *Shiny International*, no. 11 (2000).

"Spew Forth." *Walrus* 38 (2000).

"Blue Screen." *Berkeley Poetry Review*, no. 32 (1999–2000).

"Blue Screen." *Non* 2: "The Sublime" (February 1998).

Excerpt from *The Letters of Mina Harker*. *Traveling Poet*, June 1998.

> **Here, in America, at least, the Author is not dead. She is undead.**
>
> ("Undeath of the Author," 2006)

Excerpt from *The Letters of Mina Harker*. *Lipstick Eleven*, no. 1 (1998).

Excerpt from *The Letters of Mina Harker*. *14 Hills* 4, no. 1 (Fall/Winter 1997).

"Mrs. Dalloway: After Jackson Mac Low." With Joel Felix. *Chain* 4 (Fall 1997).

"Invested." *Angle*, no. 2 (June 1997).

"Invested." *Jack of Diamonds*, no. 1 (Spring 1997).

"The Flowers of Mina Harker." *Errant Bodies: Flowers*, 1996/1997.

Excerpt from *The Letters of Mina Harker*. *Open 24 Hours*, no. 12 (Spring 1996).

Excerpt from *The Letters of Mina Harker*. *Capilano Review* 2, nos. 17–18 (Winter/Spring 1996).

"The Final Letter of Mina Harker." *Red Wheelbarrow* (Santa Cruz, California) 1, no. 2 (Winter 1996).

"Dear David." *Lingo*, no. 6: *Fringe Narrative* (1996).

"An excerpt from the final letter of Mina Harker: To Laurie Weeks, October 17, 1993." *River City* 15, no. 2 (Summer 1995).

> **The committee never communicates with you directly, but gossip escapes from it like gas from a corpse, vile, dispiriting.**
>
> ("Lady Jane," 2006)

"Punctured." *Giantess: The Organ of the New Abjectionists*, no. 1 (June 1995).

"Hallucination." *Boo*, no. 4 (Spring 1995).

Excerpt from *The Letters of Mina Harker*. *Russian River Writer's Guild: Eight at Otis*, February 1995.

"Dear Reader." *Lingo*, no. 4 (1995).

"Afterwards, Falling." *publicsfear*, no. 3 (1994).

"D.B." *Some Weird Sin*, no. 2 (1994).

"Tenebrae." With Kevin Killian. *Black Bread]*, no. 4 (1994).

"Reptilicus." With Kevin Killian. *Interruptions*, no. 1 (1994).

Excerpt from *The Letters of Mina Harker*. *Inciting Desire*, no. 3 (1994).

"Dear Raymond." *Some Weird Sin*, 1991.

Excerpt from *The Letters of Mina Harker*. *Wray*, no. 4 (1993).

"To Kevin Killian, June 22, 1985." *Barscheit*, no. 3 (1992).

"Dear Patrick (October 31, 1991)." *Talisman*, no. 8 (1992).

"Dear Gail." *Sodomite Invasion Review*, no. 4 (1992).

"Hallucinations," "To Richard Hawkins," and "To Patrick Moore (March 18, 1991)." *Farm*, no. 5 (1992).

"There's Something Very Male About Me." *Bomb*, no. 36 (Summer 1991).

"To SX (Sam D'Allesandro), June 27, 1985." *Big Allis*, no. 4 (1991).

"Selections from *The Letters of Mina Harker*." *6ix*, no. 1 (1991).

"Dear Quincey." *Writing*, no. 26 (1991).

> Though I'm constantly writing about sex, increasingly what I'm interested in is not sex, but the impossibility of its representation, how physical sensation always eludes language. As Lynne Tillman's narrator says in *Motion Sickness*, "The tongue is privileged with information indifferent to words."
>
> ("Can't We Just Call It Sex?," 1998)

"I Had to Backspace, Put a Head on Every Little Person." *Gallery Works*, no. 8 (1991).

"I Was Aroused." *Zyzzyva* VI, no. 3 (1990).

"Not Clinical But Probable." *City Lights Review* 4 (1990).

"Dear Leander." *ACTS*, no. 10 (1989).

"Be My." *HOW(ever)* V, no. 3 (1989).

Excerpt from *The Letters of Mina Harker*. With Kevin Killian. *Ink*, no. 3 (1989).

"Punchline." *Athena Incognito*, no. 10 (1989).

"June 7, 1986: Dear Dr. Van Helsing." *American Poetry Archive Newsletter*, no. 42 (1989).

"September 15, 1985." *Mirage/PERIOD[ICAL]*, no. 2 (1986).

"Secret Love." *Ottotole* (1986).

"Excerpt from *The Letters of Mina Harker* (Dear Sam)." *HOW(ever)* III, no. 1 (1986).

"Complicity." *Zyzzyva* I, no. 3 (Fall 1985).

"Not Clinical But Probable." *Mirage/PERIOD[ICAL]*, no. 1 (1985).

"The Debbies I Have Known." *Feminist Studies* 10, no. 2 (Summer 1984).

"Dear Diary, Today." *Five Fingers Review*, no. 1 (1984).

CRITICAL WRITING/INTERVIEWS

Columnist. *Open Space* (blog). San Francisco Museum of Modern Art, February 2010–present.

"The Endangered Unruly: Dodie Bellamy on the Art of Mary Beth Edelson." *Artforum*, May 2019.

"Hiding in Plain Sight: Seth Price's *The World*." With Kevin Killian. www.wattis.org, January 2018. Published in conjunction with the Seth Price research season at CCA Wattis Institute for Contemporary Arts, San Francisco, September 16, 2017–July 28, 2018.

"A Conversation with Dodie Bellamy." Interview by Cori Hartwig and Estrelitta Ruiz. *Transfer* (San Francisco State University), no. 114 (November 2017).

"Sense and Sensuality." *Frieze*, August 17, 2017.

"On Being Radical." Special issue. *Purple Magazine* "On Radicality." 2017.

"A Night with Dodie Bellamy." Interview by Robert Dewhurst. "An Online Compendium and Accompaniment to *From Our Hearts to Yours: New Narrative as Contemporary Practice*." *ON Contemporary Practice*, 2017.

"What Can't Be Seen: Five Young Artists Exploring Queerness, Disability, the Standardization of Bodies and the Politics of Visibility." *Frieze*, December 29, 2016.

Interview by Lucy Ives. *The White Review*, November 2016.

"Divya Victor." *#Actual Asian Poets*, curated by Adam Fitzgerald. *Literary Hub*, October 8, 2015.

Interview by Michael Silverblatt. *The Bookworm*. KCRW, September 15, 2015.

"Adjustment Disorder: On Reading Rob Halpern's *Common Place*." *Fanzine*, September 7, 2015.

"Bookforum talks with Dodie Bellamy." Interview by Martha Grover. *Bookforum*, November 14, 2014.

"Against Easy Answers: Eating Pho with Dodie Bellamy." Interview by Lucy Tiven. *Fanzine*, October 23, 2014.

"Colonized on Every Level: An Interview with Dodie Bellamy." Interview by Christopher Higgs. *The Paris Review*, July 2014.

"On Sutures, Sutras, Cobbled Bodies and Jovian Goddesses: An Interview With Dodie Bellamy." Interview by Natalie Helberg. *Numéro Cinq* 6, no. 6 (June 2014).

"Poetry & Pornography: An Interview with Dodie Bellamy." Interview by Matias Viegener. *Los Angeles Review of Books,* February 3, 2014.

"Dodie Bellamy by David Buuck." Interview by David Buuck. *Bomb*, no. 126 (Winter 2014).

"From Cut-Up to Cunt Up: Dodie Bellamy in Conversation." Interview by Sara Wintz. *Harriet* (blog). The Poetry Foundation, 2013.

Interview by Sarah Todd. *Girls Like Giants* (blog), April 17, 2012.

Interview by Elizabeth Hall. *Denver Quarterly* 46, no. 3 (Spring 2012).

> **Kevin says that interviews are best when they are about personality. Nobody really cares about the writing; they just want to see you perform personality.**
>
> ("Dodie Bellamy by David Buuck," 2014)

"Without a net: an interview with Dodie Bellamy." Interview by Emily Gould. *Emily Books*, February 22, 2012.

"Bedside Reading: Erle Stanley Gardner and Jack Spicer." *Chicago Review* 56, no. 2/3 (Autumn 2011).

"What Is Experimental Literature? (Five Questions)." Interview by Christopher Higgs. *HTMLGiant*, June 9, 2011.

Essay. Published in conjunction with *Queer Voice*, an exhibition at the Institute of Contemporary Art, Philadelphia, April 22–August 1, 2010.

"Notes for a *San Diego Reader* Profile on Eileen Myles That Was Never Written." *Aufgabe*, no. 9 (2010).

Review of *October Country*. *Camerawork: A Journal of Photographic Arts*, Fall/Winter 2009.

"Anne McGuire's Stampede." Published in conjunction with *from Anne McGuire*, an exhibition at Marjorie Wood Gallery and an online gallery, 2008.

"A Conversation with Dodie Bellamy on Kathy Acker and Writing through the Object, the Body, and More." Interview by CA Conrad, Christina Strong, and Erica Kaufman. *PhillySound* (blog), July 2007.

"The Slit." Introduction to +|'me'S-pace, by Christine Wertheim. Los Angeles: Les Figues Press, 2007.

"Body Language." *Fascicle* 2 (Winter 2005/2006).

Interview by Jacob Evans and Matt Rohrer. *Transfer* (San Francisco State University), no. 90 (November 2005).

Interview by Jeanne Heuving. *Jacket* 2 (April 2005).

Interview by Judith Moore. *San Diego Reader*, January 13, 2005.

Interview by Julia Block. *Curve*, November 2004.

Interview by Michael Silverblatt. *The Bookworm*. KCRW, October 2004.

Interview by Brian Pera. *Suspect Thoughts*, July 2004.

"Cushman Colonials." *Nest: A Quarterly of Interiors*, Spring 2004.

Interview by Julia Bloch. *Lodestar Quarterly*, Winter 2004.

"Sylvia." *Court Green* 1 (2004).

> **My cock,**
>
> **it groweth beanshoot harde against thy softe side**
> **I am so ful of joye and of solas, hot for thee in thy rental car**
>
> (*Cunt Norton*, 2013)

Interview by Nicholas Grider. *The Nerve* (California Institute of the Arts, Valencia, California), October/November 2003.

"Assuming Risk." *NYFA Quarterly*, New York Foundation for the Arts, Winter 2003.

"Low Culture." *Narrativity*, no. 3 (2003).

"Seven Cameras and Nothing On." *Nest: A Quarterly of Interiors*, Fall 2002.

"Slits and Slashes." Interview by Mary Harron. *Nest: A Quarterly of Interiors*, Winter 2001–2002.

> **When I wore this sweater to the food stamp place, the guy gave me a month's worth without even asking to see my I.D.**
>
> ("Spew Forth," 2004)

"Class and Innovative Writing." *Lipstick Eleven*, no. 2 (Fall 2001).

"Ars Longa, Vita Brevis." *Nest: A Quarterly of Interiors*, Summer 2001.

"Sex, Body, Writing." State University of New York at Buffalo Poetics Listserv Colloquium, edited by Christopher W. Alexander. September 30, 2000.

"Mondo Mavericks Animate the Web." *ZDNet Developer*, August 25, 2000.

"Notes from the Field" and "The Demos." *Democracy the Last Campaign*. Walker Art Center, July/August 2000.

"My Mixed Marriage." *The Village Voice*, June 27, 2000.

"Class and Innovative Writing." *HOW2* 1, no. 2 (1999).

"Sponge." *Aerial*, no. 9 (1999).

Interview by Michael Silverblatt. *The Bookworm*. KCRW, October 1998.

"The Jewels of Pendom." *Speak*, Winter 1998.

"Reading Tour," *Tripwire*, no. 2 (1998).

"Can't We Just Call It Sex?" *Poetics Journal*, no. 10 (1998).

"A Poetics of Boundary Problems." *Shark*, no. 1 (1998).

"Can't We Just Call It Sex?" *Postfeminist Playground*, 1998.

"White Space." *Non* 1: "Emptiness" (October 1997–January 1998).

"Kathy Acker: an Appreciation." *The San Francisco Examiner*, December 5, 1997.

"Speaking to the Future: A Talk about Small Press Traffic." Interview by Joyce Jenkins with Robert Glück. *Poetry Flash*, November/December 1997.

"Fountain Pen Fetishists: Scratch, Scratch, Scratch." *The Stranger*, April 10, 1997.

> **In the contest of "Imagination vs. Reality," I am drawn to "versus."**
>
> ("Incarnation," 1991)

"Cold War Barbie." *Nest: A Quarterly of Interiors*, no. 1 (1997).

"Can't We Just Call It Sex?" *Writing (Post) Feminism: Electronic Book Review*, no. 3 (August 1996).

Interview by Kristin Miller. *Red Wheelbarrow*, no. 2 (Winter 1996).

"Laurie Weeks Letter to Dodie Bellamy." *Five Fingers Review*, no. 16 (December 1996).

Columnist, *Conventional Wisdom*. Xerox PARC Artist in Residence Program, August 1996.

"Summer Reading." *XXX fruit*, no. 3: "Diaries" (June 1996).

"The Fraud that is Eckankar: Hi Fubbi, this is Gakko." *San Diego Reader*, June 22, 1995.

"The Eternal Repository: An Interview with Lyn Hejinian on Letter Writing and Archiving." *Chain*, no. 2 (1995).

"The Debris of What You Really Do: A Literary Peeping Tom at UCSD." *San Diego Reader*, November 10, 1994.

Interview with Nicola Tyson. *Mirage/PERIOD[ICAL]*, no. 26 (February 1994).

"Talking on Minna Street." Interview with Andrea Juno. *Chain*, no. 1 (1994).

"Marmalade." *Avec* 7, no. 1 (1994).

Interview with Raymond Pettibon. *Shift* 7, no. 1 (1993).

"Can't We Just Call It Sex?" *Sodomite Invasion Review*, no. 5 (1993).

"Our Day with Robin Blaser." With Kevin Killian. *Lyric&*, no. 1 (1992).

"Mrs. America at the Congress of Dreams." *OUT/LOOK*, Summer 1991.

"Days without Someone." *Poetics Journal*, no. 9 (1991).

"Incarnation." *Dear World*, 1991.

"James Schuyler Gives His Second Poetry Reading Ever." *The Archive Newsletter* (The Archive for New Poetry, University of California, San Diego), no. 42 (1989).

"Digression as Power: Dennis Cooper and the Aesthetics of Distance." *Mirage/PERIOD[ICAL]*, no. 0 (1985).

Image Index

All other images throughout the publication are sourced from Kevin Killian and Dodie Bellamy Papers, Yale Collection of American Literature, Beinecke Rare Book and Manuscript Library.

Contributors

ANDREW DURBIN is the author of *Mature Themes* (2014) and *MacArthur Park* (2017), both published by Nightboat Books. He is the US Senior Editor of *Frieze* magazine and lives in New York.

KEVIN KILLIAN was one of the original New Narrative writers. He wrote three novels: *Shy* (1989), *Arctic Summer* (1997), and *Spreadeagle* (2012); a memoir; three books of stories; and four books of poetry. He co-edited *My Vocabulary Did This To Me: The Collected Poetry of Jack Spicer* (2008) and co-wrote *Poet Be Like God: Jack Spicer and the San Francisco Renaissance* (1998). Killian also wrote forty-five plays for the San Francisco Poets Theater and co-edited *The Kenning Anthology of Poets Theater 1945-1985* (2010). Other projects include *Tagged* (2012), Killian's nude photographs of poets, artists, writers, filmmakers and intellectuals; *Writers Who Love Too Much: New Narrative Writing 1977–1997* (2017), co-edited with Dodie Bellamy; *Fascination: Memoirs* (2018); and *Stage Fright* (2018). He taught writing at California College of the Arts in San Francisco.

MEGAN MILKS is a writer of fiction, nonfiction, and criticism. Their first book, *Kill Marguerite and Other Stories*, won the 2015 Devil's Kitchen Award and was named a Lambda Literary finalist. Milks is also the recipient of the 2019 Lotos Foundation Prize in Fiction Writing. They have published book and art criticism in *4Columns*, *Bookforum*, and other venues, and currently teach writing at The New School.

DR. KAYE MITCHELL is Senior Lecturer in Contemporary Literature at the University of Manchester and Co-Director of the Centre for New Writing. She is the author of two books—*A. L. Kennedy: New British Fiction* (2007) and *Intention and Text: Towards an Intentionality of Literary Form* (2008)—and editor of a collection of essays on the British author Sarah Waters (2013) and of a special issue of *Contemporary Women's Writing* (2015) on experimental women's writing. She is co-editor of *British Avant-Garde Fiction of the 1960s* (2019). Her new monograph, entitled *Writing Shame: Contemporary Literature, Gender and Negative Affect* (2020), deals with the politics and poetics of shame in contemporary literature. She is the UK editor of the *Oxford University Press* journal, *Contemporary Women's Writing*, and is on the editorial board of *Open Gender* in Germany.

Dodie Bellamy is on our mind.

This book is published in conjunction with a year-long season of
private meetings and public events about and around the work of
Dodie Bellamy. It was held at CCA Wattis Institute for Contemporary
Arts, San Francisco, from September 20, 2018 to August 14, 2019.

Editors: Jeanne Gerrity and Anthony Huberman
Design: Wayne Smith
Printing: Versa Press
Copyeditor: Victoria Gannon
Proofreader: Addy Rabinovitch
Edition: 1500
ISBN: 978-0-9802055-7-2

Dodie Bellamy Research Group: Nicole Archer, Michele Carlson,
Tonya Foster, Jeanne Gerrity, Lisa Heinis, Glen Helfand, Anthony
Huberman, Trista Mallory, Anne McGuire, K.r.m. Mooney, and
Marcela Pardo Ariza.

Between September 2018 and August 2019, Andrew Durbin gave a
lecture about Dodie Bellamy; Dodie Bellamy read from her novel-
in-progress and gave a talk about the Internet; a younger generation
of local poets and writers—Linda Bakke, Michele Carlson, Victoria
Gannon, Carlos Jackson, and Ismail Muhammad—read from their
newest work; Sara Lyons presented her stage adaptation of Kathy
Acker and McKenzie Wark's book of email exchanges *I'm Very Into
You*; Anne McGuire hosted an evening of films with Mike Kuchar;
Frances Stark discussed videos she made using sex chat rooms;